MW00454737

OPERATION GINNY

OPERATION GINNY
The Most Significant Commando Raid of WWII

VINCENT dePAUL LUPIANO

Essex, Connecticut

An imprint of Globe Pequot, the trade division of
The Rowman & Littlefield Publishing Group, Inc.
4501 Forbes Blvd., Ste. 200
Lanham, MD 20706
www.rowman.com

Distributed by NATIONAL BOOK NETWORK

British Library Cataloguing in Publication Information available

Library of Congress Cataloging-in-Publication Data

Names: Lupiano, Vincent dePaul, author.
Title: Operation Ginny : the most significant commando raid of WWII / Vincent dePaul Lupiano.
Description: Essex, Connecticut : Lyons Press, [2023] | Includes bibliographical references and
    index.
Identifiers: LCCN 2022030545 (print) | LCCN 2022030546 (ebook) | ISBN 9781493067992
    (cloth) | ISBN 9781493068005 (epub)
Subjects: LCSH: Operation Ginny, 1944. | World War, 1939–1945—Commando operations. |
    World War, 1939–1945—Campaigns—Italy. | Italy—History—German occupation, 1943–1945.
    | United States. Office of Strategic Services. | World War, 1939–1945—Secret service. | Subver-
sive activities—United States—History—20th century.
Classification: LCC D794.5 .L87 2023 (print) | LCC D794.5 (ebook) | DDC 940.54/215—
    dc23/eng/20220628
LC record available at https://lccn.loc.gov/2022030545
LC ebook record available at https://lccn.loc.gov/2022030546

To
Maryann Karinch
Always There

Much thanks to "old reliable," Stu Bran, and Stu Bran Advertising for adding to this work. You helped make the picture come alive.

War consists largely of acts that would be criminal if performed in times of peace—killing, wounding, destroying, or carrying off other people's property. Such conduct is not regarded as criminal if it takes place in the course of war, because the state of war lays a blanket of immunity over warriors.

—GENERAL TELFORD TAYLOR

Well, you know, yeah, but you cannot follow an illegal order. Trust me. There is no such thing. Not in the military. If I go into a combat situation and I tell them, "No, I'm not going. I'm not going to do that. I'm not going to follow that order," well, they'd put me up against the wall and shoot me.

—US ARMY SQUAD LEADER LAWRENCE LA CROIX,
C COMPANY, REFERRING TO HIS PARTICIPATION
IN THE MỸ LAI MASSACRE

In war, the laws are silent.

—WINSTON CHURCHILL

Contents

CHAPTER 1

"Where's the Safety Net?"

THE STORY OF OPERATION GINNY STARTS AT OLD HARBOR, BASTIA, the capital of Corsica, an island in the Mediterranean Sea west of the Italian Peninsula and immediately north of the Italian island of Sardinia. Italian and Free French forces started to push the Germans off the island after the Italian armistice in September 1943, making Corsica the first French Department to be freed.

On the afternoon of February 27, 1944, there were telltale signs of a brutal battle in Bastia: The citadel's walls were pocked with bullet holes, and the streets showed signs of shell damage. The sound of sporadic gunfire started to diminish. The Germans and the French resistance forces pursuing them were still here and there but in a dwindling capacity.

In the northeastern corner of Nouveau Port, cordoned off from the rest of the waterfront, two American patrol boats, *PT 214*, commanded by Lieutenant Koebel, and *PT 210*, were preparing to put out to sea and initiate a secret, historic mission. Navigation was left entirely to these boats' radar and compasses. Four hours and fifty minutes after departure, they arrived three hundred yards off the pinpoint. The terms "pinpoint" and "target" are often confused. A pinpoint in this context means the point onshore nearest the target; the target is self-explanatory. In the US Air Force, the pinpoint is the target—the point at which to drop bombs.

The boats were seventy-eight feet long and powered by three modified marine derivations of the 1,500 hp Packard V-12 aircraft engine, water-cooled, making 4,500 hp each. They were built by Higgins Industries and utilized an innovative V-shaped Quadraconic hull design subsequently used in later years in yachts, sailboats, and racing boats. The hull, two double diagonal mahogany planking layers, incorporated a glue-impregnated cloth layer between inner and outer planks held together by thousands of copper rivets and shiny bronze screws—one of many artisanal works of World War II equipment that can be admired today in various museums. Overall, a light and robust hull was constructed from three-thousand-year-old white cedar logs recovered from the Mountain Lake sphagnum bog in New Jersey. On January 20, 1943, they were commissioned at the Municipal Yacht Basin at Lake Pontchartrain, New Orleans. They were part of Motor Torpedo Boat Squadron Fifteen, referred to as MTBRon 15 or, as the sailors called it, Ron 15.

They were tough old gals, the first two PT boats to arrive in the Mediterranean at the end of April 1944. They fought against the Axis forces across the Western Mediterranean, North Africa, Sicily, and the southern Italian coast.

In the US Navy inventory of warships, these were the fastest boats afloat and could attain 40 knots.

The boats bristled with gunnery: two large-bore Swedish-manufactured Bofors 40mm cannons with a firing rate of 120 rounds/minute, a range of 10,750 yards, and an aircraft ceiling of 23,500 feet; it took four men to aim, fire, and load. Ammo loaded from the top in four-round clips. Each round weighed 4.75 pounds, and the projectile it fired weighed almost 2 pounds. Two twin M2 .50 caliber machine guns were mounted on turrets on the port and starboard sides. The twin-fifties were an icon of the boat's image. Crews preferred to mix armor-piercing, incendiary, and tracer ammunition firing at a rate of 730 rounds per minute. Their maximum range was 7,300 yards, and their effective range was about 2,000 yards. Mounted on the forecastle were two Oerlikon 20mm cannons. A sixty-round drum magazine mounted on the top of the gun housed the ammunition—a high-explosive tracer or incendiary round weighing approximately one-half pound. The maximum range was 4,800 yards, with a ceiling of 10,000 feet and an effective range of 1,000 yards. A gunner and a loader were needed to operate the weapon, one to cock it and fire it, and another to clear the jams that occurred. To qualify as a gunner, this team had to achieve a rate of fire between 250 and 300 yards per minute. The best crews practiced with their eyes closed to be able to perform the same tasks instinctively. Each boat had four Mark XVII torpedoes on the starboard and port sides weighing 2,600 pounds and containing

466-pound Torpex-filled warheads; Torpex was a secondary explosive, with 50 percent more knockout power than TNT. The torpedoes were known to crew members as "fish" and the torpedomen who operated them as "lovely ladies." Each vessel had a crew of fifteen to twenty sailors.

The cabin interior and exterior components were constructed of two layers of cross-hatched mahogany wood with a layer of canvas treated with anti-rot paint brushed between the planking. The cabin interior and exterior were plywood and mahogany, elegant enough to appear in *Architectural Digest* magazine.

Weight was kept to a minimum to allow for more incredible speed and maneuverability. The future president of the United States John F. Kennedy, who would be forever associated with the sinking of his PT boat—he would be blown out of the water on his *PT 109* by a Japanese cruiser—said the PT boats were "small, fast, versatile, strongly armed vessels." They could make a maximum sustained speed of 39.7 knots and a top speed of 44.1 knots with a heavy ordnance load.

Maneuverability was satisfactory, with a turning circle of 368 yards. The structural strength was also adequate, and it had a moderate tendency to "pound" in the sea. The boat, however, did have its critics. One critic, who did not "get the boat" and what it was meant to be, said the "fittings and finish were unnecessarily refined." Who did not want to go into combat in a "refined" boat? Configured as such, the cost to the US taxpayer for one shiny new seventy-eight-foot PT boat ready to sail off and sink the enemy was $206,600. Costs could ascend, of course, depending on the stack of options and configurations. By war's end, the US Navy PT boat would have more "firepower-per-ton" than any other vessel in the fleet. All the boats were painted Navy gray above and red below the waterline for camouflage. A few added a personal touch: a shark's eyes and a toothy grin on the bow, painted red, white, and blue.

The only similar boat was the German *Schnellboote* ("fast boats"), also known as *S-Boot* or *E-Boot*. They were formidable: 115 feet in length, a beam of 17 feet, a top speed of 50 knots, and 7,500 hp. The US Navy PT boat would outfire the German boat in a gunfight, but the speed differential went to the *Schnellboot*. So the idea for the PT boat was to shoot and run and leave the German boat wallowing.

Tonight, *PT 204* would have a considerable shark jaw painted around the nose on the flank—red lips and sharp white teeth; it also had shark's eyes, which gave it a menacing, pulverizing appearance. Because of this, it was nicknamed "Shark's Head." The nickname for *PT 203* was "Aggie Maru," the Corsican dialect version of Agatha Mary.

As the sun diminished behind the mountains on Corsica, Lt. (j.g.) Eugene S. A. Clifford, the senior officer in charge, began prepping for the mission; he checked each boat for anything that might be incorrect. Often, mishaps happened when loose wiring caused the navigation lights or searchlights to switch on accidentally, revealing their location to the enemy.

Tonight's mission was super stealthy: The boats would have to carry fifteen American commandos—an Organizational Group (OG) from the Office of Strategic Services, or OSS—through the darkness and travel 120 miles to the Ligurian coast and the province of La Spezia, where the Germans had a massive force of Wehrmacht troops. The OGs would disembark the PT boats, paddle to shore in bright yellow rubber boats, and blow up the tunnels. The PT boats would loiter off the coast and pick up the OGs once they completed their mission. On the way to La Spezia and back, they would have to cross shipping lanes the Germans and their *Schnellboote* patrolled regularly but not with any predictability. Thus, they had to be watchful.

As Clifford finished his inspections, two Army trucks pulled up at the dock with the fifteen commandos inside. At that moment, a light rain began; it would get heavier, and stay with them all night throughout the mission.

Unlike the subsequent Ginny II, there were nineteen OGs—fifteen enlisted men and four officers for this mission. Clifford knew most of them from prior tasks: They were known as the "Italian Operational Groups (OGs)," thus the name "Ginny." They were first- or second-generation Italian Americans from a unit formally known as Unit A, First Contingent, Operational Group, 2677th Headquarters Company Experimental (Provisional), attached to Allied Forces Headquarters. All had volunteered to join the Operational Group Command of the OSS, received basic Army training and commando training in the United States, and shipped over here. Their purposes were to sabotage operations, stir guerrilla warfare in enemy territory, and go deep behind front lines.

As soon as the OGs boarded the PT boats, 1st Lt. Albert R. Materazzi, the mission commander, instructed the enlistees to haul their weapons and equipment into the forward cabin of each boat. He gathered them in the chart house, which was the boat's nerve center. All maneuvers were directed from here by the captain or whoever was in charge of the boat at any given time. The radar display, radio communications gear, and nautical maps were in the chart house.

The OGs knew what the mission was—they had rehearsed for the last time the day before at L'Ile-Rousse, topographically like the La Spezia coast—but the officers took them through it one more time. Standing by with Materazzi and Clifford were Lieutenant (Junior Grade) Wittibort, skipper of *PT 203*; an observer, Capt. Donald B. Wentzel; and the two officers who would lead the mission: 1st Lt. and engineer Vincent J. Russo, an explosives expert from Montclair, New Jersey, and 1st Lt. Paul J. Traficante, overall commander of Operation Ginny, who would remain on one of the PT boats.

Most vital for this mission were the highly informative aerial photos taken a couple of days prior. They showed the railroad tunnel entrances—the targets—on the La Spezia–Genoa line, five hundred yards southeast of Stazione di Framura (Framura Station), the Germans' main supply line to run vital equipment and weaponry to the fighting at Cassino and Anzio. The photographs also highlighted about one thousand feet of railroad tracks between the tunnel entrances; Stazione di Framura was situated almost equidistant between the two vaulted tunnel entrances.

The mission's plan called for the PT boats to depart Bastia, land the fifteen men in their rubber boats on the craggy coastline, then loiter until the OGs completed the mission and returned to the waiting PT boats. Then they would head back to Corsica—that was the plan. It did not work out that way because of serious errors and miscalculations. Not least was navigational and disorientation among the OGs paddling ashore.

Once ashore, Lieutenant Traficante and his security party were to neutralize the railroad's signal house near one of the tunnels and then examine and evaluate both tunnel entrances and come up with a plan to blow them—and do this at a preset time. While he and one other man did this, the other members of the security party kept a lookout.

Vincent Russo and his men would go to the targets, prepare them for detonation, and then leave for the PT boats. He would not do this until he was sure the PT boats were waiting for them. Materazzi would remain with the boats, maintaining communications and updates via radio. One of the men would adjust the timers on the explosives to the time it would take for his party to leave the tunnels and get back to the boats. The explosive to be used was C4 (cyclonite, or cyclotrimethylene trinitramine), which makes up around 91 percent of C4 by mass: potent, deadly, and powerful. The plan was to cause the tunnel entrances to implode onto the tracks, which would require months of reconstruction and put the trains out of business. Once the boats left their loitering stations, the timers—according to plan—would kick off the charges at the tunnels, giving the party ample time to escape the area without engaging the Germans. Again, that was the plan. It never got that far.

Now, at the dock at Bastia, all aboard the boats took to their stations and listened to the powerful engines cough to life. They slowly moved away from the docks, their windshield wipers slashing across the rain-spattered windscreens.

"The first thing that dies in any battle is the plan of attack." So said, accurately, Carl von Clausewitz—formally, Carl Philipp Gottfried (Gottlieb) von Clausewitz—a military theorist of absolute respect, a thousand times admired. He stressed "morality" in war, or, in today's terminology, "psychology." More than anything, von Clausewitz was a realist when pondering the cannonade and splattering of body parts on the rustic hills and grassy valleys of warfare. Had he been aboard one of the PT boats right now, von Clausewitz would have allowed a faint roll of his patrician's eyes: "I am not surprised," he might have uttered.

The boats were no more than a hundred yards from the dock when Eugene Clifford announced they had to return to the dock—his radar unit was on the fritz. Hopefully it could be repaired quickly. When they got to the dock, the maintenance sailors went to work. Ten minutes later, Clifford was told that his radar unit would need a few hours to repair; they suggested he swap out *PT 203* with *PT 214*. "Shark Head" was going nowhere that night. It took about thirty minutes to transfer all the men, equipment, and weapons from *PT 203* to *PT 214*. Frustration and anxiety started to mount—and they had a strict schedule facing them when they reached the disembarkation point on the Ligurian coast.

At this point, perhaps they should have thought about delaying the mission. After all, nothing said the tunnels had to be blown that night. But they didn't delay, and that might have contributed to their failure that night. They persevered, obviously thinking they could make up the lost time. Not so.

Departure from Bastia had been scheduled for 1800 hours. It was now 1845, so they were behind schedule by forty-five minutes.

With the Packards' exhaust notes burbling, the boats forged a stable speed of 30 knots, spewing rooster tails of frothy white spray and an arrogant nose-high attitude marking their path through the chilly rain.

Leaving the Ligurian Sea, they sped into the Gulf of Genoa, the Italian Riviera—that crescent-shaped region of historic Mediterranean coastline arcing between the South of France and Tuscany—now 153 miles off their bows. The eastern half, the Riviera di Levante, is defined by rugged cliffs, turquoise coves, colorful fishing villages, and a lovely broach of cities and towns with centuries-old names: La Spezia, Portofino, Camogli, San Remo. A few miles northwest, situated in the crux of the region, Genoa, the birthplace of Christopher Columbus. The Apennine Mountains cut midsection, a range of three parallel mountains extending 750 miles along the length of Italy. In the northwest, they meld with the Ligurian Alps at Altare. They conclude at Reggio di Calabria in the southwest, the coastal city at the peninsula's tip that cups the northern portion of the horseshoe-shaped area.

At almost any other time in history, the area would be unmistakably fetching and romantic. Tonight, it could be lethal.

Pilots from the Eighth Air Force had flown reconnaissance missions and delivered photographs of the target. After studying the photos, it was decided that the original 375 pounds of explosives would be more effective if increased to 600 pounds.

Fifteen miles northwest of La Spezia, the two tunnels sat on opposite ends of the small railroad station named Stazione di Framura (Framura railway station) and Bonassola, a small fishing village. Occasionally, writers and historians mark the forces' landing point as La Spezia and other as Bonassola because they are close. The tunnels were on the railroad line—the only one—that *Generalfeldmarschall* (General Field Marshal) Albert Kesselring liked to use to transport supplies to his embattled troops in the north, specifically the Cassino area of northern Italy.

OSS intelligence agents had obtained construction documents of the tunnels. They spent time interviewing engineers from the maintenance section of the Italian railways about the tunnels near Framura. If the tunnels were imploded onto the tracks, all rail transportation—all the Wehrmacht's vital supplies—would cease rolling for many months, starving an irreplaceable supply chain and shutting down the entire German offensive in Italy.

⁓

So far in this war, various departments of the executive branch, including the State, Treasury, Navy, and War Departments, had been conducting intelligence and commando activities ad hoc, with no overall direction, coordination, or control. The sloppy manner of operating displeased President Franklin Roosevelt. He asked US Army colonel William Joseph "Wild Bill" Donovan to draft a plan for an intelligence service modeled on the British Secret Intelligence Service (MI6) and Special Operations Executive. On July 11, 1941, Donovan accepted President Roosevelt's appointment as Coordinator of Information (COI) for the OSS.

Donovan was an excellent choice. He had graduated from Columbia Law School and was a decorated veteran of World War I. The only person to receive four of the United States' highest awards—the Medal of Honor, Distinguished Service Cross, Distinguished Service Medal, and National Security Medal—he also received the Silver Star and Purple Heart, as well as decorations from several other nations.

Because of Donovan's background, education, and well-connected aristocratic friends, the OSS was quickly referred to as the "office of social service." Soon a storied list of Ivy Leaguers joined the OSS ranks.

Julia Child—yes, *that* Julia Child (née McWilliams): 1934 graduate of one of the Seven Sisters, Smith College, with a BA in history. Deemed too tall at six feet, two inches, Child's attempted enlistment was rejected by the Women's Army Corps (WAC) and the US Navy's WAVES. Undeterred in her desire to serve her country, the future celebrity chef and TV cooking host began an OSS career as a typist at OSS headquarters in Washington, DC. She then was assigned as an assistant to the team that developed shark repellent to ensure that curious sharks would not explode ordnance targeting German U-boats. When Child was asked to solve the shark attacks, she started experimenting with "recipes" that were distasteful to curious sharks. Still in use today, Child's recipe foray into a functional shark repellent led to her formulating some of today's tastiest recipes, writing numerous cookbooks, and blazing the trail for many soon-to-follow TV cooking shows. Her efforts would earn her the OSS's lauded Emblem of Meritorious Civilian Service. Child's award cited her numerous personal virtues, including her "drive and inherent cheerfulness." (And you thought she was only a celebrity chef!)

Ralph Bunche, Harvard; political activities: a BA from UCLA and a PhD from Harvard. Bunche was a political scientist, academic, and diplomat. In 1950 he received a Nobel Peace Prize for his late 1940s mediation on Israel—the first African American to be so honored. In 1963 Bunche was awarded the Presidential Medal of Freedom by President John F. Kennedy. Bunche retired, unannounced, from his position at the UN. He died on December 9, 1971, at age sixty-eight and is buried in Woodlawn Cemetery in the Bronx, New York City.

Arthur Goldberg, Associate Justice of the US Supreme Court, US Secretary of Labor, sixth US Ambassador to the United Nations; graduate of Crane College and DePaul University, and recipient of a Doctor of Jurisprudence degree from Northwestern University. Frustrated with the war in Vietnam, Goldberg resigned from the ambassadorship in 1968 and accepted a senior partnership with the New York law firm Paul, Weiss, Rifkind, Wharton & Garrison. A former member of the US Army, Ambassador Goldberg is buried in Arlington National Cemetery in Washington, DC.

Arthur Meier Schlesinger Jr., American historian, social critic, public intellectual; Harvard College graduate, 1938. Attached to the OSS from 1943 to 1945.

John Martin "Jack" Feeney Ford, film director (*Stagecoach, The Man Who Shot Liberty Valance, The Grapes of Wrath*) and winner of six Academy Awards. Ford served in the US Navy (1942–1945) and the US Naval Reserve (1946–1962). He achieved the rank of commander (active) and rear admiral in the Naval Reserve. He was in the Battle of Midway and the Battle of Normandy. His Navy awards, sixteen, are too numerous to spell out here. At the age of seventy-nine, Ford died at Palm Desert, California, and is buried at Holy Cross Cemetery in Culver City, California.

———

Donovan began his new assignment by quickly establishing the groundwork for a centralized intelligence program. He organized COI's New York City headquarters in Room 3603 at Rockefeller Center in October 1941, a few stories above the rehearsal hall—where the world-famous Rockettes were *tap-tapping* their high-kicking routines to perfection. He had asked Allen Dulles, future director of the CIA, to head the COI; the offices Dulles took were on the floor immediately above the location of the operations of Britain's MI6. The nearby presence of the Rockettes was a pleasant diversion from the deadly business going on above their heads.

In 1942 COI ceased being a White House operation and was put under the authority of the Joint Chiefs of Staff. Roosevelt also changed COI's name to the Office of Strategic Services, which, in the years to follow, would evolve into the Central Intelligence Agency.

So, there they were: two sophisticated spy agencies, a flank of long-legged, high-stepping dancers, and the Easter Bunny—all in one world-famous building in midtown Manhattan. The kids and their families in the audience below had no idea.

After the OSS formed into an agency, it began coordinating espionage activities behind enemy lines for all branches of the US Armed Forces. Functions included the use of propaganda, subversion, and post-war planning. It was said that an OSS candidate was "a Ph.D. who could win a bar fight." In its time, the OSS was indeed the tip of the spear that defended America, and its influence is still seen today throughout the intelligence community.

———

The OSS espionage and sabotage operations demanded highly specialized equipment. General Donovan called in experts, organized workshops, and funded labs that later formed the core of the Research & Development Branch. Stanley P. Lovell, a Boston chemist, became the first head of this department. Donovan called him "Professor Moriarty."

Throughout the war years, the OSS R&D adapted Allied weapons and espionage equipment. They produced a line of customized spy tools and gadgets, including silenced pistols, lightweight submachine guns, "Beano" grenades that exploded upon impact, explosives disguised as lumps of coal ("Black Joe") or bags of Chinese flour ("Aunt Jemima"), acetone time-delay fuses for limpet mines, compasses hidden in uniform buttons, playing cards that concealed maps, a 16mm Kodak camera in the shape of a matchbox, tasteless poison tablets ("K" and "L" pills), and cigarettes laced with tetrahydrocannabinol acetate (an extract of Indian hemp) to induce uncontrollable chattiness.

The OSS also developed innovative communication equipment such as wiretap gadgets, electronic beacons for locating agents, and a device called "Joan-Eleanor," a portable radio system that made it possible for operatives on the ground to establish secure contact with a plane that was preparing to land or drop cargo. OSS R&D also printed counterfeit German- and Japanese-issued identification cards and various passes, ration cards, and money.

On August 28, 1943, Stanley Lovell was asked to present in front of a hostile Joint Chiefs of Staff. They were skeptical of OSS plans beyond military intelligence and were ready to split the OSS between the Army and the Navy.

While explaining the purpose and mission of his department and introducing various gadgets and tools, Lovell dropped into a wastebasket a Hedy—a panic-inducing explosive device in the shape of a firecracker, which shortly produced a loud shrieking sound followed by a deafening boom. The presentation was interrupted and did not resume, since everyone in the room had fled. In reality, the Hedy, jokingly named for Hollywood movie star Hedy Lamarr for her ability to distract men, later saved the lives of some trapped OSS operatives.

Not all of Lovell's projects came to fruition. Many ideas were odd—such as a failed attempt to use insects to spread anthrax in Spain. Later, Lovell said, "It was my policy to consider any method whatever that might aid the war, however unorthodox or untried."

At Camp X, near Whitby, Ontario, Canada, an "assassination and elimination" training program was operated by the British Special Operations Executive, assigning exceptional masters in the art of knife-wielding combat, such as William E. Fairbairn and Eric A. Sykes, to instruct trainees. Many members of the OSS also were trained there. It was dubbed "the school of mayhem and murder" by George Hunter White, who taught at the facility in the 1950s.

From these nascent beginnings, the OSS began to take charge of its destiny and opened camps in the United States and finally abroad. Prince William Forest Park (then known as Chopawamsic Recreational Demonstration Area) was the site of an OSS training camp from 1942 to 1945. Area C, comprising approximately six thousand acres, was used extensively for communications training; Area A was used for training some of the OGs. Catoctin Mountain Park, now the location of Camp David, was the site of OSS training Area B, where the first Special Operations (SO) were trained. Special Operations was modeled after Great Britain's Special Operations Executive, which included parachute, sabotage, self-defense, weapons, and leadership training to support guerrilla or partisan resistance. Considered most mysterious of all was the "cloak and dagger" Secret Intelligence, or SI branch. Secret Intelligence employed "country estates as schools for introducing recruits into the murky world of espionage. Thus, it established Training Areas E and RTU-11 ('the Farm') in spacious manor houses with surrounding horse farms." Morale Operations training included psychological warfare and propaganda. The Congressional Country Club (Area F) in Bethesda, Maryland, was the primary OSS training facility. The Catalina Island Marine Institute Facilities at Toyon Bay on Santa Catalina Island, California, are composed (in part) of a former OSS survival training camp. The National Park Service commissioned a study of OSS national park training facilities by Professor John Chambers of Rutgers University.

The main OSS training camps abroad were located initially in Great Britain, French Algeria, and Egypt; later, as the Allies advanced, a school was established in southern Italy. In the Far East, OSS training facilities were established in India, Ceylon (now Sri Lanka), and then China. The London branch of the OSS, its first overseas facility, was at 70 Grosvenor Street, W1. In addition to training local agents, the overseas OSS schools also provided advanced training and field exercises for graduates of the training camps in the United States and for Americans who enlisted in the OSS in the war zones. The most famous of the latter was Virginia Hall in France.

Since 1943, the 2677th had been headquartered and operational at L'Ile-Rousse, Corsica. They had been actively harassing German-held coastal targets and blowing up communication lines throughout Italy from Cassino to Anzio.

The Allied forces recognized that the main German supply route was the railway line running along the snaking western coast of Italy. The Allied air forces had been conducting Operation Strangle to cut all German routes of communication; however, bombing in the mountainous terrain along the craggy coast had not cut the Genoa-Livorno line. It stood, almost impervious to countless pounding by US bombers. The OSS and Allied forces knew that, as the main transport, Genoa-Livorno was vital. Shut that down, and German operations would slam to a halt.

But blowing up railroad tracks and signal stations was relatively easy and not an effective long-term action: Twisted railroad tracks could easily be repaired and put back into service within days, sometimes hours, which frustrated the Allies.

The OSS started looking for a "magic pill"—they almost certainly do in situations like this—an effective military remedy that would destroy the railroad tracks that transported Wehrmacht troops, equipment, and supplies to the ongoing battle in the north against the Americans. Airpower was neither severe enough nor accurate enough in the mountainous terrain to achieve that goal. And the notion of a commando raid went to Colonel Glavin.

Edward J. F. Glavin—born and raised in New York City, a 1927 graduate of West Point—was an Army public-relations officer stationed in Brooklyn, New York, in September 1943 when he was sent on a secret mission overseas. He was put in command at the OSS headquarters at L'Ile-Rousse. He directed and oversaw missions of 2,800 agents from all the armed services throughout Africa, France, Italy, and the Balkans.

Not long after he arrived, Allied G-3 Special Operation presented Glavin with a bold plan that, if successful, could sever the Genoa-Livorno railroad line. Glavin was receptive, even eager.

G-3 proposed a sabotage party of commandos to blow up two train tunnels on the line. About fifteen miles northwest of La Spezia, the two tunnels between Stazione di Framura and the small fishing village of Bonassola were deemed the most promising target. The saboteurs would leave from the island of Corsica aboard two PT boats then disembark onto dinghies (rubber boats), paddle to shore, and make their way to the tunnels.

G-3 didn't expect Galvin's reaction.

"Where's the safety net?" he asked, scanning the room for an answer. There was none.

"Last year," he told the group, "a woman hoarder filled her cellar with canned goods. As soon as she was done marking the last can, a rainstorm flooded the cellar and washed all the labels off the cans."

Everyone in the room got the colonel's point; that's why he was a colonel.

Glavin knew there was no "safety net" once the men landed onshore. This had to have been one of the first flaws in their plan—particularly regarding the lives of the men.

Once the men were ashore, the PT boats could not loiter; there were constant German patrols. After the men had been dropped off to carry out the mission, they were on their own; the boats would return the following day (if they could). If they successfully blew up the tunnels, the fifteen American soldiers still had to get back to the shore, launch the rubber boats, and paddle out to the PT boats.

The plan, they thought, had a reasonable chance of success. As presented, Ginny I's overall plan had been considered reasonably pragmatic, and despite the odds—not ideal—Glavin gave his approval.

First, all commandos had to volunteer for Operation Ginny. Like all unit members, A/1st Contingent all were soldiers who had completed basic Army training before being accepted as volunteers in Operational Groups. All knew the unique demands for operating behind enemy lines in Italy. For nearly a year, Unit A Contingent had been training to carry out particular operations to help support local partisans and such raid and sabotage operations as Ginny. They rehearsed at night on the rocky western coast of L'Ile-Rousse, where the topography was similar to tonight's pinpoint target.

Emilio T. Caruso, a former OG officer in Unit A and later battalion adjutant in a special reconnaissance battalion, wrote the following about Unit A's training program:

> Since all OGs were recruited from the Army, it was assumed that they had completed basic training. This gave the organization a head-start, and OG training was specialized in nature, with particular emphasis on physical condition. Courses were designed to make all OGs proficient in demolition, small arms, both American and foreign makes, scouting, patrolling and reconnaissance; first-aid, unit security measures; living off the land; hand-to-hand combat and fighting with a knife, camouflage, map-reading, and compass use; and the equipment and methods of airborne and seaborne raids. A great many of the tactical exercises were conducted at night. Operational training included mountain operations, parachuting, amphibious operations, skiing, light artillery, radio operations, and advanced espionage tactics. The aggressiveness of spirit and willingness to close with the enemy were stressed.

Despite this, their training had been inadequate compared to subsequent Italian, French, German, Greek, Norwegian, and Balkan OGs, said one veteran of the first Ginny operation.

To have qualified, the Ginny OGs had to be of Italian American heritage and had to speak either fluent or partial Italian. One spoke fluent Genovese, the prevalent dialect in this area. They had been trained in overt activities, particularly demolitions, assassinations, intelligence gathering, hand-to-hand combat, and sabotage. Their objective would require a complex formula of timing, courage, audacity, numerous details, and an abundance of luck.

—◦—

At about 2230 hours, another obstacle arose.

The PT boats' radar screen picked up hits that could have been enemy vessels—specifically, the fast-moving, lethal German *Schnellboote*. The PT boats were about four miles from the coastline and could make out lights. From here, the boats went into "silent mode": Each muffler had butterfly flap valves fitted in the main exhaust that ran the usually loud exhaust down through the muffler and under the water line. Usually, this was only done at low speeds.

The OGs came out of their reverie and began gathering their equipment and blowing up the two rubber boats. Lieutenant (Junior Grade) Clifford set a course for Stazione di Framura. His calculations were only made through the cockpit instruments and the onboard maps. This form of navigation was probably responsible for his missing the pinpoint, because in 1944 there was no such thing as GPS. Clifford was up against a moonless night, near-zero visibility, and light rain.

At this point, the only distinguishable objects onshore were two mountains to the north. Since that might have "appeared" to be the pinpoint area, Clifford headed the boats in their direction.

At 2230 hours, Vincent Russo, standing with Clifford in the cockpit, told Clifford he believed they were heading in the wrong direction. Clifford ordered a course change again, heading them south—until they came to Scoglia Ciamia and stopped.

Russo and his men started to disembark. When all the men and equipment were aboard the rubber boats, Russo gave Materazzi his best salute, unhooked the lines, and pushed off the PT boat. The OGs started paddling to the shore; the serious part of the mission had begun.

No one among them was calm; there were a lot of butterflies. They all knew that several mistakes, miscalculations, and errors had already been made—most important, they were now ninety minutes off schedule. The combination of the errors, the darkness, and the rain just added to their trepidation. All knew that for a mission to go well, it had to run like clockwork; tonight was running like a clock, only this one was broken. They could not get the ninety minutes back. They could not stop the rain. They could not guarantee the pinpoint. The only thing to do was move forward and pray things would somehow fall into place. But at this point, they knew they were against stiff odds.

Aboard the PT boats, the gunners were on high alert for enemy vessels.

At 0145 Materazzi's radio came alive with Russo's voice saying they had followed Materazzi's direction and found the fissure that would lead them up the cliff. Russo said he would personally inspect the area and report back. Meanwhile, the clock kept ticking. Russo climbed the fissure to the top of the cliff, nearly falling several times because the rain made the rocks slick as ice. As soon as Russo reached the top of the cliff, he heard a train northwest of where he was standing. He took a deep breath, knowing he was in trouble. Again, he realized they were in the wrong spot. At 0245 he radioed Materazzi and asked for permission to remain ashore and make another attempt the next time.

Aboard *PT 214*, Materazzi and Eugene Clifford started to make calculations; they told Russo to stand by while they tried to figure things out.

According to their mission timetable, they should have been leaving the coastline with the OGs at 0330—this would provide cover from the overcast skies and the rain. They told Russo that they could only loiter until 0400 at the latest, then they had to leave for Bastia. If they waited any longer, it would be daylight, the weather could worsen, they could be exposed to German patrols, and would generally be way off the timetable and in serious jeopardy of losing control of the whole mission. It could evolve into a deadly situation.

Materazzi concluded that it would take Russo and his men until 0530 to reach the tunnels—and then they would need thirty minutes to set the time fuses and attach the C4 to the tunnel openings. When Materazzi rolled this over in his mind, he ordered Russo and his men to return to the PT boats. By 0315 the OGs were aboard the PT boats and heading for Bastia, where they arrived at 0730.

The next day, the following report was disseminated:

Office of Strategic Services

Operation Group

Mission: To interdict the Genoa–La Spezia rail line which was the main supply route for supplies, weapons and armaments to the Cassino front and the Anzio bridgehead, by sabotaging two tunnel entrances southeast of the Framura rail station and booby trapping the open rails between them.

Summary:

1. Departed Bastia harbor on February 27 1944 at 1845 aboard two PT boats delayed by 45 minutes because the lead boat with the working party on board had to be replaced due to a faulty radar. Lt. Harold Nugent, commanding the replacement, had no knowledge of the mission and only after clearing the mine fields was told to head to within four miles of the Framura station where the OSS personnel would take over the navigation.

2. February 28 1944 at 0125 they were three hundred yards from the shore and began debarking and completed ten minutes later. Lt. Materazzi watching their progress by binoculars and radar noted they were drifting southeast of the target and to turn northwest. At 0200 Lt. Russo, commanding the shore group radioed that they were landing.

3. At 0245, having left the personnel on the shore, he had climbed to the target and reported that it would take another 1.5 hours to complete the mission and return to the PT boats. He requested permission to remain to prepare the charges and complete the mission the following night. Lt. Materazzi noting that time was running out and the possibility that weather or other factors might not permit a return told him to abort the mission and return to the PT boats. Re-embarkation completed 0315.

4. They arrive in Bastia at 0730. The mission is postponed until the next month.

CHAPTER 2

Führerbefehl (Leader Order)

DIEPPE, A COASTAL COMMUNE IN THE SEINE-MARITIME DEPARTMENT in the Normandy region of northern France, is a distant but significant aspect of the execution of the Ginny commando raids. Dieppe and Operation Ginny would extend into the future of WWII and beyond and influence the Nuremberg Trials beginning in November 1945—both would rewrite the rules of warfare.

The Dieppe Raid, or Operation Jubilee, was a costly battle for the Allies.

On August 19, 1942, Allied soldiers, mainly drawn from the 2nd Canadian Infantry Division, landed at Dieppe in the hope of occupying the town for a short time to gain intelligence and draw the Luftwaffe into open battle. The conflict that ensued was deadly. And there were more prisoners taken than the American Army experienced in the eleven months of the 1944–45 Northwest Europe campaign. (And no major objectives were achieved.) More recent research suggests the raid was a massive cover for an intelligence operation to capture German code machine components—a story for another day.

Profound repercussions began on the same day of the raid, August 19.

Against explicit orders, a Canadian brigadier took a copy of the operational order ashore. The order was subsequently discovered on the beach by the Germans and found its way to Hitler. Among the dozens of pages was an instruction to "bind prisoners." The orders, misinterpreted by German intelligence, were meant for the Canadian forces, *not* the commandos. Bodies of shot German prisoners with their hands tied were allegedly found by German troops after the battle.

On October 3–4, 1942, ten men of the Small Scale Raiding Force and No. 12 Commando (attached) made an offensive raid, Operation Basalt, on the German-occupied isle of Sark. The objective was to reconnoiter the island and capture prisoners. The Sark commandos took five German prisoners. One guard remained with the captives, and the commandos tied the German prisoners' hands behind their backs to minimize the guard's task. The commandos stated that one of the German captives began shouting to alert his comrades in a nearby hotel. He was immediately shot dead. The remaining prisoners were silenced by stuffing their mouths with grass and dirt.

Three of the four remaining captives made a break for the beach. It has never been proven if they freed their hands before or during the escape. In any event, one was shot and another stabbed. A third did manage to escape, but the fourth was conveyed safely back to England.

A few days after the Sark raid, the Germans issued a communiqué claiming that at least one German prisoner had escaped and two had been shot while attempting to escape, having had their hands tied; the Germans contended that the "hand-tying" practice had also been used at Dieppe.

Hitler was fuming over the treatment of his troops and sought draconian revenge. On October 7, Hitler personally penned a *Führerbefehl*—a Leader Order—and passed it on to the Wehrmacht Daily Communiqué, the Wehrmacht High Command's mass-media report and a critical component of Nazi propaganda during WWII:

> In the future, all terror and sabotage troops of the British and their accomplices, who do not act like soldiers but rather like bandits, will be treated as such by the German troops and will be ruthlessly eliminated in battle, wherever they appear.

Two days later, October 9, Berlin announced that 1,376 Allied prisoners (mainly Canadians captured at Dieppe) would henceforth be shackled. The Canadians responded with a similar-in-practice shackling of German POWs in Canada.

German High Command (OKW) lawyers, officers, and staff quickly crafted Hitler's Leader Order (*Führerbefehl*) into the draconian

Commando Order (*Kommandobefehl*) Number 46: "Instructions for Intensified Action Against Banditry in the East." Initially, on October 18, 1942, only twelve copies were issued and classified top secret.

The order contained an appendix stating that it was "intended for German commanders only and must not fall into enemy hands under any circumstance." The fact that Hitler's staff took exceptional measures to keep the order secret, including the initial printing of only twelve copies, strongly suggests that they knew the Commando Order to be illegal and would be internationally condemned. Still, having to comply with the Führer's wish, they gave no pushback.

The order in its entirety stated:

The Führer   SECRET

No. 003830/42g. Kdos. OWK/Wst. FH Qu 18.10.1942. 12 copies.
For a long time now, our opponents have been employing in their conduct of the war, methods which contravene the International Convention of Geneva. The members of the so-called Commandos behave in a particularly brutal and underhanded manner, and it has been established that those units recruit criminals not only from their own country but even former convicts set free in enemy territories. From Captured orders, it emerges that they are instructed not only to tie up prisoners, but also to kill out-of-hand unarmed captives who they think might prove an encumbrance to them or hinder them in successfully carrying out their aims. Orders have indeed been found in which the killing of prisoners has positively been demanded of them.

In this connection, it has already been notified in an Appendix to Army Orders of 7.10.1942 that in future, Germany will adopt the same methods against these Sabotage units of the British and their Allies; i.e. that, *whenever they appear, they shall be ruthlessly destroyed by the German troops* [emphasis added].

I order, therefore: From now on all men operating against German troops in so-called Commando raids in Europe or in Africa, are to be annihilated to the last man. *This is to be carried out whether they be soldiers in uniform, or saboteurs, with or without arms; and whether fighting or seeking to escape; and it is equally immaterial whether they come into action from Ships and Aircraft, or whether they land by parachute. Even if these individuals on discovery make obvious their intention of giving themselves up as prisoners, no pardon is on any account to be given* [emphasis added]. On this matter, a report is to be made on each case to Headquarters for the information of Higher Command.

Should individual members of these Commandos, such as agents, saboteurs, etc., fall into the hands of the Armed Forces through any means—as, for example, through the police in one of the Occupied Territories—they are to be instantly handed over to the SD.

To hold them in military custody—for example in POW Camps, etc.—even if only as a temporary measure, is strictly forbidden.

This order does not apply to the treatment of those enemy soldiers who are taken prisoner or give themselves up in open battle, in the course of normal operations, large-scale attacks; or in major assault landings or airborne operations. Neither does it apply to those who fall into our hands after a sea fight, nor to those enemy soldiers who, after air battle, seek to save their lives by parachute.

I will hold all Commanders and Officers responsible under military law for any omission to carry out this order, whether by failure in their duty to instruct their units accordingly, or if they themselves act contrary to it.

The next day, Jodl issued twenty-two copies with the following addendum:

HEADQUARTERS OF THE ARMY   SECRET

No. 551781/42G.K. Chefs W.F.St/Qu. FH Qu. 19/10/42. 22 Copies. Copy No.21.

The enclosed order from the Führer is forwarded in connection with destruction of enemy Terror and Sabotage troops.

This order is intended for commanders only and is in no circumstances to fall into Enemy hands.

Further distribution by receiving Headquarters is to be most strictly limited.

The Headquarters mentioned in the Distribution list are responsible that all parts of the order, or extracts taken from it, which are issued are again withdrawn and, together with this copy, destroyed.

Chief of Staff of the Army
(Sgd.) JODL

According to the OKW, this order was issued in retaliation for the Germans' opponents "employing in their conduct of the war, methods which contravene the Third Geneva Convention, specifically 'relative to the Treatment of Prisoners of War'" (first adopted in 1929, with the last revision in 1949).

How ironic: The Allies were accusing the Germans of "contravening the Geneva Convention" by mishandling and executing captured Allied soldiers. Simultaneously, the Germans were accusing the Allies of contravening the Geneva Convention regarding the treatment of German POWs. There is no question, however, that atrocities, including murder, were committed by both the Allies and the Germans. These commando killings started in late 1942 and continued through the war.

The first victims were two officers and five other ranks of Operation Musketoon, who were shot in Sachsenhausen on the morning of October 23, 1942.

In November 1942, British survivors of Operation Freshman were executed.

In December 1942, Royal Marine commandos captured during Operation Frankton were executed under this order. After a naval firing squad executed the captured Royal Marines in Bordeaux, the Commander of the Navy, Admiral Erich Raeder, wrote in the *Seekriegsleitung* war diary that the executions of the Royal Marines were something "new in international law, since the soldiers were wearing uniforms." American historian Charles Thomas wrote that Raeder's remarks about the executions in the *Seekriegsleitung* war diary seemed to be and might have reflected a bad conscience on the part of Raeder.

On July 30, 1943, the captured seven-man crew of the Royal Norwegian Navy motor torpedo boat *MTB 345* were executed by the Germans in Bergen, Norway.

On January 1944, British Lt. William A. Millar escaped from Colditz Castle and vanished; it is speculated that he was captured and killed in a KZ camp.

After the Normandy landings, thirty-four SAS soldiers and a USAAF pilot captured during Operation Bulbasket were executed. Most were shot, but three were killed by lethal injection while recovering from wounds in a hospital.

The Commando Order was invoked to facilitate the death of an unknown number of Allied special operations forces and behind-the-lines operators such as the OSS (Office of Special Operations), the SOE (Special Operations Executive), and other special forces elements. "Commandos" of those types captured were sent to German security and police forces and transported to concentration camps for execution. In this case, the *Sicherheitsdienst* (Security Service)—*Sicherheitsdienst des Reichsführers–SS*. This "handing over," according to Hitler's direction, meant that the captured commandos, saboteurs, and others were handed over to the SD and would inevitably be sent to a concentration camp (aka KZ) and executed.

The matter had now escalated into a stalemate of sorts—but in this case, one with deadly consequences for the fifteen Ginny commandos who were among the first Americans to fall victim to Hitler's outrage.

It was abundantly clear to the Germans that failure to carry out Hitler's Commando Order by any German commander or officer would be considered an act of blatant negligence punishable under German military law. The death penalty would not be off the table.

First, every German soldier knew that it was a crime to obey an illegal order, but many looked the other way. Not all German soldiers and officers accepted the Commando Order with blind obedience, even enthusiasm. Some generals, such as *Generalfeldmarschall* Erwin Rommel, never relayed the order to their subordinates. Although some officers were horrified when they heard of the order, most officers—particularly those in the Waffen-SS, the armed component of the SS—did carry it out.

Rommel and *Generalfeldmarschall* Gerd von Rundstedt were "old school" officers who had almost no respect for Adolf Hitler. At his trial for war crimes in Nuremberg, von Rundstedt said something that opposed the draconian measures Hitler was taking to win the war: "As a senior soldier of the German Army, I will say this: We accused leaders were trained in the old soldierly traditions of decency and chivalry. We lived and acted according to them, and we endeavored to hand them down to the younger officers. However, Hitler disagreed."

(**Note:** Hitler's Commando Order was the second commando order. Von Rundstedt had submitted the first on July 21, 1942; it stated that parachutists should be handed over to the *Geheime Staatspolizei* [Secret State Police, aka Gestapo]. This meant a certain death sentence.)

At the Nuremberg Trials, the Commando Order was asserted as a direct breach of the laws of war, and German officers who carried out illegal executions under the Commando Order were found guilty of war crimes and sentenced to death or, in two cases, extended incarceration.

During WWII, atrocities were not confined to the Wehrmacht and showed an imbalance. If attention is focused solely on Hollywood movies and innumerable books on the subject, massacres, crimes, brutalities, and outright murders and rapes were committed almost exclusively by the Germans—specifically the Waffen-SS, the most notorious organization of the German Army. Scant attention, however, has been given to crimes committed by the US Army. Such a notion makes us uneasy; it opposes the idea and image of "the greatest generation." The Germans, the Waffen-SS, on the other hand, were the enemy "you loved to hate."

In her book *Looking for the Good War: American Amnesia and the Violent Pursuit of Happiness*, Elizabeth D. Samet writes that "treatments of World War II have done real harm, distorting our understanding of the past and consequently shaping how we approach the future."

If the execution of the twelve Ginny commandos was a war crime, so were many similar actions by Americans.

To learn how hypocritical we were as a nation, we would have to wait twenty-five years, for the Mỹ Lai massacre and the mass murder and rape of unarmed South Vietnamese civilians by US troops in Son Tinh district, South Vietnam, on March 16, 1968.

There, between 347 and 504 (the count has never been certified) unarmed people were killed by US Army soldiers from Company C, 1st Battalion, 20th Infantry Regiment, and Company B, 4th Battalion, 3rd Infantry Regiment, 11th Brigade, 23rd (Americal) Infantry Division. The number killed, the way they were killed, and who killed them is an inconceivable crime on a scale of unprecedented mass murder.

The following is a disposition of the officers and enlisted men who participated in the massacre at Mỹ Lai, which most of them got away with.

Officers

First, before being shipped to South Vietnam, all of Charlie Company's soldiers—enlisted men and officers—went through advanced infantry training and basic unit training at Pohakuloa Training Area in Hawaii. At Schofield Barracks, they were taught how to treat POWs and distinguish VC guerrillas from civilians by a Judge Advocate. So, they knew the rules before shipping out.

Lt. Col. Frank A. Barker commanded Task Force Barker, a battalion-sized unit, assembled to attack the VC 48th Battalion supposedly based in and around Mỹ Lai. He allegedly ordered the village's destruction and supervised his helicopter's artillery barrage and combat assault. Barker reported the operation as a success and was killed in Vietnam on June 13, 1968, in a midair collision before the investigation into the massacre had begun.

Capt. Kenneth W. Boatman was a forward artillery observer. The Army accused him of failure to report possible misconduct; the charge was dropped.

Maj. Charles C. Calhoun, operations officer of Task Force Barker. Charges against him for failure to report possible misconduct were dropped.

Lt. Col. William D. Guinn Jr., Deputy Province Senior Advisor/ Senior Sector Advisor for Quang Ngai Province. Charges against him of dereliction of duty and false swearing brought by the Army were dropped.

Col. Oran K. Henderson, the 11th Infantry Brigade commander, ordered the attack and flew in a helicopter over Mỹ Lai during the massacre. After Hugh Thompson immediately reported multiple killings of civilians, Henderson started the cover-up by dismissing the allegation about the massacres and reporting to superiors that twenty people from Mỹ Lai died "by accident." He was accused of cover-up and perjury by the Army, but the charges against him were dropped.

MSgt. G. Samuel W. Kester, commander of the 23rd Infantry Division, was not planning the Mỹ Lai search-and-destroy mission. However, he flew over Mỹ Lai in a helicopter during the operation and monitored the massacre via radio communications. Afterward, Kester did not follow up with the 11th Brigade commander, Col. Oran Henderson, on the initial investigation. Henderson was later involved in the cover-up. Subsequently, the Army charged him with failure to obey lawful regulations, dereliction of duty, and alleged cover-up. Charges were dropped, but he was later stripped of a Distinguished Service Medal.

Capt. Eugene M. Kotouc, military intelligence officer assigned to Task Force Barker, provided partial information on which the Mỹ Lai combat assault was approved. Together with Capt. Ernest Medina and a South Vietnamese officer, he later interrogated, tortured, and allegedly executed VC and NVA suspects. He was charged with maiming and assault and tried by a jury. Outcome: acquitted.

Capt. Dennis H. Johnson of the 52nd Military Intelligence Detachment, assigned to Task Force Barker, was accused of failure to obey lawful regulations. Charges were later dropped.

Second Lt. Jeffrey U. Lacross, platoon leader, 3rd Platoon, Charlie Company, testified that his platoon did not meet any armed resistance in Mỹ Lai and that his men did not kill anybody. However, since in his words both Calley and Brooks reported a body count of sixty for their platoons, he then submitted a body count of six.

Maj. Robert W. McKnight, operations officer, 11th Brigade. Accused of false swearing by the Army. Charges were subsequently dropped.

Capt. Ernest Medina, commander of Charlie Company, 1st Battalion, 20th Infantry. Nicknamed "Mad Dog" by subordinates, he planned, ordered, and supervised the operation in Son Mỹ village. He was accused of failing to report a felony and of murder and went to trial. Acquitted.

Capt. Earl Michaels, Charlie Company's commander during the Mỹ Lai operation, died in a helicopter crash three months later.

Brig. Gen. (one star) George H. Young Jr., at the time, the assistant division commander, 23rd Infantry Division. Charged with the alleged cover-up, failure to obey lawful regulations, and dereliction of duty by the Army. Charges dismissed.

Maj. Frederic W. Watke, commanding officer, Company B, 123rd Aviation Battalion, 23rd Infantry Division, providing helicopter support on March 16, 1968. Testified that he informed Col. Henderson about killings of civilians in Mỹ Lai as reported by helicopter pilots. Accused of failure to obey lawful regulations and dereliction of duty. All charges dropped.

Capt. Thomas K. Willingham of Company B, 4th Battalion, 3rd Infantry Regiment, assigned to Task Force Barker. Charged with making false official statements and failure to report a felony. Charges were dropped.

Altogether, fourteen officers, directly and indirectly involved with the operation, including two generals, were investigated in connection with the Mỹ Lai massacre. Lt. Col. Frank A. Barker, Capt. Earl Michaels, and 2nd Lt. Stephen Brooks died before the investigation.

1st Platoon, Charlie Company 1st Battalion 20th Infantry

Pfc. James Bergthold Sr., assistant gunner and ammo bearer on a machine gun team with Sp4 Robert E. Maples, was never charged with a crime. He admitted that he killed a wounded woman he came upon in a hut "to put her out of her misery."

Pfc. Michael Bernhardt, a rifleman, had dropped out of the University of Miami to volunteer for the Army. He refused to kill civilians at Mỹ Lai. Capt. Medina later reportedly threatened Bernhardt to deter him from exposing the massacre. In retaliation, Bernhardt was given more dangerous assignments, such as point duty on patrol, and as a direct result would contract a form of trench foot. Bernhardt told Ronald Ridenhour, who was not present at Mỹ Lai during the massacre, about the events, pushing him to continue his investigation. Later, he would help expose and detail the massacre in numerous interviews with the press. He served as a prosecution witness in the trial of Medina, where he was subjected to intense cross-examination by defense counsel F. Lee Bailey. Bernhardt is a recipient of the New York Society for Ethical Culture's 1970 Ethical Humanist Award.

Pfc. Herbert L. Carter, aka "Tunnel Rat," shot himself in the foot while reloading his pistol to be medevaced out of the village when the massacre started.

Pfc. Dennis L. Conti, grenadier/minesweeper, testified that he initially refused to shoot but later fired some M79 rounds at a group of fleeing people with unknown effect.

Sp4 Lawrence C. La Croix, squad leader, testified favorably for Capt. Medina during his trial. In 1993 he sent a letter to the *Los Angeles Times*, saying, "Now, 25 years later, I have only recently stopped having flashbacks of that morning. I still cannot touch a weapon without vomiting. I am unable to interact with any of the large Vietnamese population in Los Angeles for fear that they might find out who I am; and because I cannot stand the pain of remembering or wondering if maybe they had relatives or loved ones who were victims at Mỹ Lai. Some of us will walk in the jungles and hear the cries of anguish for all eternity."

Pfc. James Joseph Dursi, rifleman, killed a mother and child then refused to kill anyone else, even when ordered to do so by Lt. William L. Calley.

Pfc. Ronald Grzesik, a team leader, claimed he followed orders to round up civilians but refused to kill them.

Sp4 Robert E. Maples, machine gunner attached to SSgt. Bacon's squad. He stated that he refused to kill civilians hiding in a ditch and claimed his commanding officer threatened to shoot him.

Pfc. Paul D. Meadlo, rifleman, said he was afraid of being shot if he did not participate. Lost his foot to a land mine the next day. Later, he publicly admitted his part in the massacre.

SSgt. David Mitchell, squad leader, was accused by witnesses of shooting people at the ditch site. Pleaded not guilty. Acquitted.

Sp4 Charles Sledge, radiotelephone operator, was a prosecution witness.

Pfc. Harry Stanley, grenadier. Claimed to have refused an order from Lt. Calley to kill civilians rounded up in a bomb crater but refused to testify against Calley after he was featured in a documentary and several newspapers. Berkeley, California, designated October 17 as Harry Stanley Day.

Sgt. Esequiel Torres. Previously Torres had tortured and hanged an old man because Torres found his bandaged leg suspicious. He and Sgt. Gary D. Roschevitz were shooting a group of ten women and five children in a hut. Calley ordered Torres to man the machine gun and open fire on the grouped villagers. Torres ceased fire before everyone in the group was down and refused to fire again. Calley took over the M60 and finished shooting the remaining villagers in that group himself. Torres was charged with murder. Acquitted.

Sp4 Frederick J. Widmer, assistant radiotelephone operator. Widmer, the subject of pointed blame, is quoted as saying, "The most disturbing thing I saw was one boy—and this was something that, you know, this is what haunts me from the whole, the whole ordeal down there. And there was a boy with his arm shot off, shot up half, half hanging on, and he just had this bewildered look in his face and like, 'What did I do, what's wrong?' He was just, you know, it's hard to describe, couldn't comprehend. I, I shot the boy, killed him, and it's—I'd like to think of it as a mercy killing, because somebody else would have killed him in the end, but it wasn't right." Widmer died on August 11, 2016, at age sixty-eight.

OTHER SOLDIERS

Nicholas Capezza, chief medic, HHQ Company. Insisted he saw nothing unusual that day.

William Doherty and Michael Terry, 3rd Platoon soldiers who participated in killing the wounded in a ditch.

Sgt. Ronald L. Haeberle, photographer, Information Office, 11th Brigade, attached to Charlie Company. Then-Sergeant Haeberle carried and operated two cameras during the operation: an official US Army-issued camera using black-and-white film, which was submitted as part of the report in process to brigade authorities, and a privately owned camera loaded with color film. Haeberle, by his testimony at his court-martial, admitted that official photographs did not include soldiers committing the killings and generally avoided identifying the individual perpetrators. The color camera, however, contained numerous images of soldiers killing older men, women of various ages, and children. Haeberle also testified that he had destroyed most of the color slides that incriminated individual soldiers because he believed it was unfair to blame only these individuals when many more were equally guilty. He attempted to sell these photographs to US newspapers on his return home and was subsequently investigated by the US Army. Considerable criticism has been leveled at Haeberle for remaining silent during the initial attempts at covering up the incident when he had enormous evidence in his possession, as well as his later seeming attempts to benefit financially from the sale of this evidence.

Sgt. Minh Duong, Army of the Republic of Vietnam (ARVN) interpreter, 52nd Military Intelligence Detachment, attached to Task Force Barker. He confronted Capt. Medina about the number of civilians who were killed. Medina reportedly replied, "Sergeant Minh, don't ask anything—those were the orders."

Sgt. Gary D. Roschevitz, grenadier, 2nd Platoon. According to the testimony of James M. McBreen, Roschevitz killed five or six people standing together with a canister shot from his M79 grenade launcher, which had a shotgun effect after exploding. He also grabbed an M16 rifle from Pfc. Varnado Simpson to kill five Vietnamese prisoners. According to witnesses, he later forced several women to undress in order to rape them. When the women refused, he reportedly shot at them.

Pfc. Varnado Simpson, rifleman, 2nd Platoon, admitted that he killed around ten people in Mỹ Lai on Capt. Medina's orders to destroy not only people but *even cats and dogs*. He fired at a group of people where he allegedly saw a man with a weapon but instead killed a woman with a baby. He committed suicide in 1997 after repeatedly acknowledging remorse for several murders in Mỹ Lai.

Sgt. Kenneth Hodges, squad leader, was charged with rape and murder during the Mỹ Lai massacre. In every interview, he strictly claimed that he was following orders.

———

American troops were indeed involved in committing war crimes during World War II. But none—at least none reported—was more heinous than the Mỹ Lai massacre. And if they were committed, many went unpunished or were passed over by American commanders—as is evidenced by the results of the courts-martial of the Mỹ Lai participants.

Many American soldiers who had been in Mỹ Lai during the massacre accepted personal responsibility for the loss of civilian lives. Some of them expressed regrets without acknowledging personal guilt. For example, Ernest Medina, Company's C's commander, said, "I have regrets for it, but I have no guilt over it because I didn't cause it. That's not what the military, particularly the United States Army, is trained for."

In 2010, Lawrence La Croix, a squad leader in C Company, stated, "A lot of people talk about Mỹ Lai, and they say, 'Well, you know, yeah, but you cannot follow an illegal order.' Trust me. There is no such thing. Not in the military. If I go into a combat situation and I tell them, '*No, I'm not going. I'm not going to do that. I'm not going to follow that order,' well, they'd put me up against the wall and shoot me*" [emphasis added].

In almost every case, the participants in the massacre were following illegal orders—sometimes clear and direct, other times implied—to kill unarmed civilians at the direction of their superiors. It is moot as to whether or not they believed the orders to be illegal—the fact is, they obeyed a wholly criminal order.

WILLIAM LAWS CALLEY JR.

Lt. William Laws Calley Jr. was more prominent than any other soldier involved in the massacre. He was the main focus of the press, public opinion, and the US military criminal proceedings. After deliberating for seventy-nine hours, the six-officer jury (five of whom had served in Vietnam) convicted Calley on March 29, 1971, of the premeditated murder of twenty-two South Vietnamese civilians. On March 31, Calley was sentenced to life imprisonment and hard labor at Fort Leavenworth, Kansas. Calley was the only soldier convicted out of the twenty-six officers and enlisted men initially charged for their part in the Mỹ Lai massacre or the subsequent cover-up. Many observers saw Mỹ Lai as a direct result of the military's attrition strategy, with its emphasis on body counts and kill ratios.

Multiple trials and hearings for Calley over time revealed that the public would not accept that their soldiers—Calley in particular—could commit such a murderous, medieval massacre as Mỹ Lai. They simply would not accept the details. Their boys didn't do that.

Many participants at Mỹ Lai refused to testify against Calley. One who did testify was Pfc. Paul David Meadlo, who had been granted immunity. Ordered to testify or face contempt-of-court charges, Meadlo recounted explicit, heinous details of what had happened as he stood guard over some thirty villagers that he, along with Pvt. Dennis Conti, had gathered at a defoliated area at the hamlet's southern tip. He stated that Calley approached him and told him: "You know what to do with 'em." Meadlo misinterpreted the order to mean only to keep watch over the villagers. However, when Calley returned ten minutes later, he was enraged to see that the villagers—men, women, children, and babies—were still alive. After telling Meadlo that he had wanted them dead, Calley backed up about twenty feet, lowered his M16, let loose with a full magazine, and ordered Meadlo to join in. Meadlo obeyed the order and then proceeded to round up more villagers to be massacred.

Calley was a war criminal convicted by court-martial for the deliberate killings of two hundred to four hundred unarmed South Vietnamese civilians. Nevertheless, three days after his conviction, President Richard Nixon released him to house arrest. A new trial was ordered by the United States Court of Appeals for the Fifth Circuit, but that ruling was overturned by the United States Supreme Court. Calley served three years of house arrest for the murders. Public opinion about Calley remained divided.

—✦—

The closest the US Army came to Mỹ Lai in WWII happened on July 14, 1943, almost a year before the launch of Ginny II.

US troops, led by incensed US Army Colonel George Herbert McCaffrey, fired on looters in what is called the Canicatti (Italy) massacre, killing eight civilians in less than eight painfully murderous, blood-spilling, brain-splattering minutes.

The town of Canicatti had already surrendered when US troops entered, following heavy German bombardment during their withdrawal. US troops received a report that civilians were looting a bombed factory and filling buckets with the factory's stores—food and liquid soap.

At around six o'clock on a muggy, starless evening, Lt. Col. McCaffrey, the military governor of Palermo, and several of his battle-battered US military police arrived at the factory in a particularly agitated, blood-thirsty state, with safeties off their weapons and fingers poised on their triggers.

McCaffrey quickly drew his sidearm, an M1911 Colt .45 automatic pistol, from its leather holster, cocked a round into the pipe, and fired into the unruly crowd after it had failed to obey his shrill order to cease and disperse.

Some said they heard Italians cursing at him in Italian:

The Italians yelling, "*Vaffanculo!*" ("Fuck you!")

Others heard shouts of "*Vai a farti fottere!*" ("Go fuck yourself!")

What ensued was sudden, deadly, and profoundly criminal. At least eight civilians went down, killed, including an eleven-year-old girl, although the exact number of casualties is uncertain.

The Canicatti massacre (aka Canicatti Slaughter) was unquestionably a war crime, but McCaffrey was neither charged nor designated a war criminal. No charges were drawn against him, nor were any of his enthusiastic military police classified as war criminals—after all, they were obeying the orders of their commanding officer. McCaffrey, a lieutenant colonel and clearly in command of his troops, gave the order to fire, and his boys obeyed with grim enthusiasm.

Should all who had obeyed McCaffrey, including McCaffrey, have been arrested, tried for war crimes, and potentially executed? If the Allies had lost the war and the tables been turned, McCaffrey and his troops would undoubtedly have been tried and convicted. McCaffrey verbally issued an illegal order, and his troops obeyed that illegal order—no question at all. What would have happened to them had they *not* followed their commanding officer? Would they have been put up against a stone wall and executed? Disobeying an order in the US military is a serious offense, particularly one that leads to a crime.

In the case of *General der Infanterie* (Lieutenant General) Anton Dostler, the situation was like the Canicatti massacre. Obeying Hitler's *Führer befehl*, Dostler passed what he believed to be a legal order down through his chain of command (he was, after all, following his oath to the Führer and the Führer's Commando Order). Dostler was undoubtedly privy to the Commando Order because of his rank and position; he freely admitted it. How far could this responsibility be taken? What about Dostler's staff, who passed the order down the chain of command? What about the members of the firing squad who executed the Ginny OGs? Were they not also guilty of obeying an illegal order? Where does this end?

Was "victor's justice" at play here for McCaffrey? Yes.

Attorney General William Barr set off a firestorm after dismissing all charges against former national security advisor Gen. Michael Flynn. He then added more fuel to the fire when *CBS News*'s Catherine Herridge asked him, "When history looks back on this decision, how do you think it will be written?"

"Well," Barr replied, "the winners write history, so it largely depends on who's writing the history."

Barr was in good company. Winston Churchill has similarly said, "History is written by the victors."

The rules were starting to change, and those involved in Ginny would soon find how significant and deadly the change would be and how impactful it would be on the Nuremberg Trials.

On the same date as the Canicatti incident, July 14, 1943, *two* US Army massacres occurred simultaneously at the Regia Argonautica's 504 Air Base in Santo Pietro, a small village near Caltagirone, in southern Sicily. It is called the Biscari massacre, singular, but it was two atrocities at the same place on the same date. There, US troops of the 180th Infantry killed seventy-one Italian and two German POWs in the two incidents. In the first incident, thirty-seven Italians and two Germans were killed; thirty-six Italians were killed in the second incident.

The 180th Infantry Regiment had faced punishing resistance near the Santo Pietro airfield. By 10:00 a.m., the Americans had taken several prisoners, including forty-five Italians and three Germans. The Americans were agitated and aching for revenge.

Maj. Roger Denman, executive officer for the 1st Battalion, 180th Infantry Regiment, ordered Sgt. Horace T. West, thirty-three years old, to take the prisoners to the rear, off the road, where they would not be conspicuous, and hold them there for questioning. The POWs were without shoes and shirts, which was common to discourage escape attempts. Whether they took their shirts and shoes off themselves or were ordered to do so by Sergeant West is unknown.

After Sergeant West, with several other US soldiers assisting him, marched the POWs about a mile, he halted the group and directed eight or nine to be separated from the rest and escorted to the regimental intelligence officer (the S-2) for questioning. West then took the remaining POWs off the road, lined them up, and borrowed a Thompson submachine gun from the company's first sergeant. When asked what he wanted the Thompson for, West said, "To kill the sons of bitches." West then told the soldiers guarding the POWs to "turn around if you don't want to see this."

West then let loose with the Thompson, killing the thirty-seven remaining POWs. The bodies were discovered thirty minutes later. Each POW had been shot through the heart, indicating close range. Investigators later learned that after West had emptied the Thompson into the group of POWs, he had stopped, reloaded, and then walked among the prisoners lying in their pooling blood, firing a single round into the hearts of those still moving.

The next day, the thirty-seven bodies caught the attention of a chaplain, Lt. Col. William E. King. He reported the event to his senior officers, who at first dismissed it because of the "bad press" the matter would receive "if it went public." Still, after some convincing, they agreed to take the incident to court, accusing West of murder.

The US Army charged Sgt. Horace T. West with "willfully, deliberately, feloniously, [and] unlawfully" killing thirty-seven prisoners of war. At his trial, which began on September 2, 1943, West pled not guilty. Although he admitted to the killings, his non-lawyer defense counsel raised two matters in his defense:

First, West was "fatigued and under extreme emotional distress" at the time of the killings and was essentially temporarily insane. However, 1st Sgt. Haskell Y. Brown testified that West had borrowed the Thompson and an additional magazine of thirty rounds and had appeared to act in cold blood.

Second, West's counsel stated that he was *simply following the orders of his commanding general* (Omar Bradley). West claimed that Bradley, in a speech to his troops before the invasion of Sicily, had said that "prisoners should be taken only under limited circumstances." This "wink of the eye" and "glancing the other way" indicated that POWs could be executed on the spot. What else could it mean? And should not Bradley also have been court-martialed?

West's regimental commander, Col. Forrest E. Cookson, testified that General Bradley had also said that if the enemy continued to resist after US troops had come within two hundred yards of their defensive position, "surrender of those enemy soldiers need not be accepted." The problem with this defense was that the prisoners had already surrendered at Santo Pietro, and the surrender *had* been accepted. Thus, they should have been classified as prisoners of war.

The court-martial panel found West guilty of premeditated murder, stripped him of his rank, and sentenced him to life imprisonment. He was detained in North Africa for fear that his presence in federal prison could bring unwanted publicity to him and his crime. On reviewing West's record of the trial, Gen. Dwight D. Eisenhower, future president of the United States, decided to "give the man a chance [for killing thirty-seven POWs]" because West had "served enough of his life sentence to demonstrate that he could be returned to active duty."

After West's brother wrote to the Army and his local US representative, it was decided to "resolve the worrisome matter," and on the recommendation of the War Department's Bureau of Public Relations, the deputy commander of Allied Headquarters in Italy signed an order remitting West's sentence on November 24, 1944. Restored to active duty, West received an honorable discharge at the end of the war. He died in January 1974, age sixty-three, and is buried in Lakeview Cemetery in Love County, Oklahoma.

When he was informed of the massacres, Gen. Omar Bradley told Gen. George Patton—old "blood and guts"—that US troops had murdered some fifty to seventy prisoners in cold blood. Patton, in his diary, wrote his response:

> *I told Bradley that it was probably an exaggeration, but in any case* [emphasis added], to tell the officer to certify that the dead men were snipers or had attempted to escape or something, as it would make a stink in the press and would make the civilians mad. Anyhow, they are dead, so nothing can be done about it.

Essentially, General Patton asked General Bradley to lie about killing thirty-seven people, indicating that he did not want to be bothered with the seventy-one slaughtered soldiers and civilians in Biscari. Bradley, thankfully, refused Patton's suggestions. Patton later changed his mind. After learning that the 45th Division's inspector general had found "no provocation on the part of the prisoners . . . they had been slaughtered," Patton was reported to have said, "Try the bastards."

The US Army ultimately chose to do nothing because it would be "bad press"; besides that, their fighting men were not monsters, arbitrarily murdering unarmed prisoners—only the Japanese and the Germans were doing that.

Between the Biscari massacres in 1943 and November 1945, there were twenty-one mass killings throughout Italy. Of those, three were committed by US troops. One of those, the bombing of Gorla in October 1944, was conducted by the US Army Air Force. USAAF bombers hastily discarded their bombloads on a densely inhabited area. Among those killed were 184 pupils of the Gorla elementary school. No one was charged with a criminal act.

CHAPTER 3
Capture

Ginny I's plan was considered generally sound enough to be used for the second attempt to blow up the tunnels approximately one month later.

First of all, despite their unsuccessful attempt on February 27, 1944, the Ginny OGs were determined to get the job done and now had more knowledge and experience regarding the overall mission. Yes, things would be better the second time out, they felt. They practiced getting in and out of the PT boats and into the rubber boats until they could do it with their eyes closed; they went through inflating the boats and anything else related to the sea trip that had to be done with precision. They checked their weapons so many times they thought they would wear them thin. They thought they had a better shot at blowing the tunnels than they did the first time. The experience had been a good teacher. Even more than before, they had the spirit they needed to succeed. Their next target date would be March 22, and they would put the time to good use.

OSS agents in Naples "obtained" the tunnels' construction documents, and interviewed engineers from the construction crews. They then went to pilots of the Eighth Air Force and obtained photographs, studied them over and over, and asked the pilots to go up and shoot another batch for them. All this information was new and helped them better understand the topography around the tunnels.

Vincent Russo, the mission's engineer, studied all the latest information. He concluded that instead of using 375 pounds of C4, 650 pounds would be better—half for one tunnel, the other half for the second tunnel. He and the rest of the OGs rehearsed this at L'Ile-Rousse, a location on the island of Corsica opposite Bastia, similar to La Spezia. At night on March 20, two days before the raid date, they made a dry run.

The PT boats would arrive at the disembarkation point, a cove below Capeneggio three hundred yards southwest of the pinpoint. Once there at 2300 hours, March 22, the shore party would transfer from the two PT boats to the three rubber dinghies. They would follow a ravine, or fissure, that extended 150 meters to the open section of the railroad track and the tunnel openings on either side of Stazione Framura and neutralize the signal house, or linesman's shed. There, at 0300 hours on March 23, they would commence work.

Lieutenant Traficante would lead the security party, head toward the signal house, and neutralize it. Included in his party were Technical Specialists Grade 5 (T/5s) Joseph Noia, Rosario F. Squatrito, and Storo Calcara. They would do an immediate reconnaissance of the targets and then pass along the signal to proceed to Lieutenant Russo.

Upon receiving the signal, Russo and his party would set the charges. With him were Sgt. Alfred L. De Flumeri, Sgt. Dominick C. Mauro, and T/5s Liberty J. Tremonte, Joseph J. Leone, Thomas N. Savino, and Joseph A. Libardi. However, if Russo determined that the explosives could not be set on time, he would signal Materazzi, telling him they would be back on the boats by 0300. Some of the party would remain onshore, hide during the day, and then, at 2300 hours the next night, with only two men at the tunnels, finish setting the C4. Only after contact with the PT boats with a red "R" signal would they initiate the C4 charges—weather permitting. All this depended on the PT boats' ability to return the following night and loiter until the OGs came aboard.

It is important to note here that all the OGs of the working and security parties were dressed in regulation uniforms of the US Army. Some German reports stated that some, if not all, of the OGs were not in US Army uniforms and were instead dressed in civilian clothes or did not have US Army insignia. This was patently false and, at the trial of *General der Infanterie* (General of the Infantry) Anton Dostler, would be ineffectively proposed in the general's defense. In other words, said the prosecution, treating the OGs as spies was illegal because they were dressed as US Army commandos.

(*Note:* This is an important point of law regarding the treatment of prisoners of war versus spies. A POW is an enemy combatant dressed in his country's uniform who has either surrendered voluntarily or is forced to surrender. A spy is an individual dressed in civilian clothes or dressed in the uniform of his enemy who is deliberately hiding his identity and thus has an "unfair"—if one can use that word—advantage. The handling of spies versus POWs falls under different rules of warfare, as we shall see later.)

The Ginny OGs wore woolen OD shirts and trousers when they departed Bastia. Cascara, Tremonte, and Farrell wore paratrooper boots; the others wore GI shoes with canvas leggings. Some of them were wearing OD sweaters. All had either the old-type jackets or the new pile type, which they wore inside out to eliminate the shine. All wore knit stocking caps. Insignia and rank were worn on their shirts or jackets, although Materazzi had removed his captain's bars and left them in the desk drawer of his office in Bastia. All the OGs wore dog tags around their necks except Lieutenant Traficante. They all had the Model 1911 Colt .45 automatic pistol in regulation leather holsters. All carried Fairbairn-Sykes fighting knives inserted through the space between the back of the holster and the hanger, which connected the latter to their pistol belts. Six of the OGs carried 9 mm Marlin submachine guns with extra ammunition, similar in design to the Thompson submachine guns.

———

At 1755 hours on March 22, 1944, the PT boats departed Bastia, arriving at Stazione Framura at 2245 hours; they had come within three hundred yards of the shore. Ten minutes later, the OGs had inflated the rubber boats, had them in the water, loaded the C4, shoved off from the PT boats, and headed for shore. So far, no glitches. But the night was young.

At 2315 hours the shore party sent a garbled message to Materazzi; there was no response. Ten minutes later, Russo got on the radio and said he was at the shoreline looking for a spot to land the rubber boats. Materazzi replied, "OK." Ten minutes later, Russo was on the radio again to Materazzi, saying he thought he had found the target. Materazzi did not know what this meant. Thirty minutes later, Russo radioed Traficante , saying, "We see you. Wait for us." That was the last communication from the Ginny fifteen.

Almost at that moment, several *Schnellboote* were running at the PT boats at high speed. As a diversionary tactic, one of the PT boats broke off, taking enemy fire from the lead *Schnellboot*. By now, Materazzi's PT boat had drifted two miles from its loitering spot and waited five hundred yards offshore. But Materazzi had been spotted from the shore: A green flare shot up and outlined his PT boat. Then, from the sea came a red flare, a response to the green light, clearly showing the outline of Materazzi's PT boat. Materazzi thought he saw machine-gun fire coming at them from the shore, but the bullets were splashing too far off their bow to be effective.

Materazzi quickly determined this was not a good spot for the PT boats. He ordered both to head west for five miles. Once there, they would join up, turn around, head back to where they had been, and try to reestablish a connection with the shore party.

At 0200 hours the rendezvous was successful, but more *Schnellboote* appeared simultaneously. The PT boats effectively initiated evasive maneuvers, and one hour later the *Schnellboote* were gone.

But misfortune struck again.

One of the PT boats had a serious problem, actually, two problems: Both the main and auxiliary steering mechanisms were not functioning, and both boats had to wait while the malfunctions were repaired. It was now 0415, too late for the boats to return to the pinpoint, retrieve the OGs, and get out of there before sunrise.

Materazzi held a meeting with the other boat's skipper. They concluded it would be best to go back to Bastia and return the next night, as per the contingency plan, and off they went back to their home base in Bastia.

The PT boats returned to the pinpoint on March 23, but before they reached it, their radar indicated several large enemy craft at sea. They were blocked from making shore and the pinpoint. From where they were, they saw blinking lights coming from the shore—a possible enemy trap to lure them. With no way they could loiter, they headed back to Bastia. A photo reconnaissance mission flown the next morning revealed no damage to the tunnels and no sign of the OGs. The Ginny OGs had not succeeded in blowing the tunnels. But where were they?

A final attempt was made on the night of March 25, but again there was no sign of the OGs. That was the end of the attempts to bring them home. Initially, the OSS listed them as missing in action; later, as captured by the enemy.

From here, events become debatable, often confusing, and conflicting. There is of course no rendering on the part of the OGs as to what they endured—no record of their communications or the decisions they had to make. Once they left the shoreline and proceeded up the cliff, the last communication Lt. Materazzi heard was, "We are here. Come to us."

So, what happened to the Ginny OGs after they landed?

After the OGs left the PT boats on March 24, they paddled to the shore to discover sheer cliffs rising formidably, straight from the sea. They moved up the coast to seek a more suitable place. The rough seas complicated their rowing and the direction they were heading. Several OGs fell into the water and had to swim to shore, and they lost fifteen cases of C4 explosives.

The mission was deteriorating with alarming speed. What to do?

Once ashore, they discovered they were in the wrong spot. Traficante tried to reconnect with Materazzi—no luck. The walkie-talkies had been ruined. Russo decided that demolishing the tunnels was out of the question, at least tonight. As dawn approached, the OGs pulled the rubber boats up about 50 feet from the beach and set out to camouflage them. The entire party of OGs then went about four hundred yards uphill until they found an abandoned barn, where they decided to hide for the day.

Partial communications from the OGs and reports from local Italians and Germans provide a less-than-clear picture of their arrival at the pinpoint and ascent up the fissure.

In May, the end of the war in Italy in sight, Capt. Lawrence R. Houston, OSS theater legal counsel, met with representatives of the Judge Advocate General's Office. He advised Colonel Glavin, commanding a force of 2,800 agents in France, Africa, Italy, and the Balkans, of the investigations of war crimes allegedly perpetrated against OSS personnel. Shortly afterward, two officers were assigned to investigate: Lt. (j.g.) Kelly O'Neill Jr., USNR, and 1st Lt. Robert Blythin. Their assignment: "to proceed with and coordinate the investigation of alleged war crimes against OSS personnel of the Mediterranean Theater." They would liaise with the War Crimes Board of the Judge Advocate General. Lt. Blythin focused his attention on Ginny—soon discovering the contributions made by earlier OSS investigators.

Once ashore, the OGs had attempted to camouflage the dinghies with leaves, tree limbs, and brush; the attempt was inept. Yes, the dinghies could not be seen from the cliff above, but they could be seen from the sea, and a fisherman reported them. Further, the rubber boats were bright orange. (Why would the powers that be have permitted that color for the boats?) This set off an immediate German and partisan search.

More than anything else, bungling the camouflaging of the rubber boats was probably the OGs, biggest mistake and would, sadly, lead to their capture.

The only helpful information at this time regarding the OGs came from the enemy's intercepted telex reports and communiqués monitored by the BBC in London. Using the sparse details from enemy telex communiqués, this is what occurred immediately after the OGs landed.

While the records of *Brigade Almers* could not be found, the war diary (*Kriegstagebuch*) of LXXV Army Corps showed that the Ginny OGs were captured midmorning on March 24. The enemy's GSO (intelligence office) entry stated:

Mar. 44: 500 meters west of Bonassola (22 kilometers northwest of La Spezia), an American sabotage team consisting of two officers and thirteen NCOs and other ranks, landed and were slaughtered (*abgeschlachtet*) by troops of Fortress Brigade for Special Use stationed there.

The GSO's report was only partially correct—the OGs had not been *slaughtered*—and the hour and day were not recorded. Instead, the OGs had been captured but were still alive.

Information gathered by OSS Captains Lanier and Manzini during an interview of an eyewitness recorded on May 5 provided essentials in reconstructing the movement of the Ginny OGs on March 23 and their capture the next day.

The witness was a sixteen-year-old herdsman, Franco Lagaxo, who lived with his mother near Carpeneggio—a locality on Monte Pastorelli four hundred meters northwest of Bonassola and southeast of the Framura station. Young Lagaxo's deposition was taken at the Carpeneggio town hall. He spoke clearly and simply, without elaboration or artifice. He did not have a vested interest in the matter, which could have motivated him to lie. He did not face any criminal charges so was not trying to make a deal for himself. Nor could he profit from falsifying or embellishing his account. Lagaxo's rendering is essential for understanding what happened to the OGs during the last thirty-four hours of their lives. Here is a verbatim translation:

On March 23, 1944, around 0900 hours, I was in the vicinity of my house when I noted two armed men in military uniform who were asking about us. They asked my mother and I, too, went into the house. The two soldiers identified themselves as American, and [upon entering] the house placed themselves near the fire [,] as they were wet. They immediately told me to say nothing and [asked] if I could bring them to the "little house" of the railroad. I told them "Yes," and after about 5 minutes we left. Following the path of the woods, I accompanied them to the locality of Paggio, which is about 800 meters from my house, and in about 10 minutes, we arrived [at] the place. They immediately told me that it was not what they were seeking, [*sic*] and leaving me free, they charged me with buying them fish, eggs, and wine and said they would return to get them at my house. The soldiers remained [at] the place, and I returned home and, given some money, I went into town where I bought fifteen eggs and a liter of wine. Bringing the purchase home, I remained there to wait, and about noon, they returned, three of them, the two of the morning and another. They entered the house and ate with us some "polenta" and after having taken the eggs and the wine they left again agreeing that about 15 hours I would go to get them, near a little stable which is about 200 meters from my house to accompany them to [another] "little house." At 15 hours, I went to the place, and together with all three, I conducted them above the second "little house," [which required about an hour's walk to reach it]. Upon arrival, they said, "This is the place where we were supposed to land." After about 15 minutes, they told me I could leave, and they remained on the spot. They were speaking with each other in American, and I could not understand anything. I returned home, leaving them alone. In the evening towards dusk I noted the same two . . . were seated about 50 meters from my house. On the morrow [March 24] at about 0800 hours, while I was going fishing, I saw in the distance the Americans who were climbing from the sea towards the house. Arriving at the rocks, I noted some fisherman gathering material, and I noted that with them was the Fascist Bertone. Instead of fishing, I returned home, and I found the two Americans by the door . . . waiting for mother. I asked them if they had left the material on the rocks, informing them that Fascists were taking it in the boat. They answered "Yes" and said they were leaving because they were causing too much bother, and my mother arriving at that time gave them some bread and jam. Out of curiosity, I then went to the mule trail that leads to the town, and I saw a group of Germans and Fascists who were coming up. On my own initiative, I ran to the little stable to warn the Americans, and for the first time, I saw that they were a numerous group. I turned back, taking another path, and I met the Fascists Bertone and Ferri who asked me if I had seen any-one. I answered "no" and despite their insistence I stayed on the negative. The Fascists proceed and in the vicinity of my house the groups of German and other Fascists dispersed. I, from the vicinity of the house, watched to see what would happen, and after several minutes I saw that the two Fascists Bianchi and Bertone were about 15 meters above a small grove where were hiding the two Americans I knew. Bertone then yelled to them, "What are you doing here, ugly pigs." The two answered, "We are Italians." Bertone added, "you are traitors." In that moment, Bianchi threw a hand grenade and then asked where the other [*sic*] were. Having received a reply that there was no one else, Bertone said, "Do you want to bet that if I blow the whistle, the others will come out?" He emitted a whistle and almost immediately [yelled] in Italian, "Here they are!" I, however, from my position, did not see them. In the meantime, I head shooting with machine gun [*sic*] and rifles but only for a short while. After a little time, I saw coming towards my house the group of Americans with their hands raised surrounded by Fascists and two Germans. The others continued to search the vicinity and towards 1100 hours they returned, taking away with them the Americans imprisoned in the storehouse. While they were leaving, the Fascists Bertone and Bertine were saying that they had made a good catch, adding that they had taken the English and that we never saw anything. In the evening, the Germans came for the guard, and they asked me if I had seen someone else and if it were true that I was feeding them. I denied everything, and on the following day, I was interrogated by Commissioner of the Commune [*sic*] Guglielmini to whom I always denied having seem them. (Signed) Lagaxo Franco. Bonassola, May 5 1945.

While the above statement offers a general idea of how the OGs were captured, it does not offer an explanation as to why they gave up so easily—a bothersome question that has been debated for many, many years and an action for which the OGs have long been criticized. Only speculation can approach an answer. Russo knew the area was covered with Germans and Fascists and that it would be difficult to elude them. He also knew that if they did manage to get back to the rubber boats, where would they go? The PT boats were not loitering, not waiting for them. And since their radios had been ruined, there was no way of communicating with friendly forces.

Russo knew he was in a difficult, if not impossible, position and probably figured that the odds were against them—they were. The idea of a clean escape without bloodshed looked ridiculous because they were outgunned in a foreign land and without any form of backup. But countless Americans—not present at that moment, of course—would have liked to have seen the fifteen Italian Americans at least try to fight their way out of an ugly confrontation and have them shed their blood to the last man, the last bullet. That's what Americans did, after all, and nothing less would suffice. Of course none of these critics were on-site the moment the Germans appeared with their machine pistols and hand grenades. Further resistance would only have produced bloodshed and loss of lives; Russo knew this for sure. It was one thing to go down with the ship, another to die without a sense of achievement. Besides, Russo knew the rules of engagement, the treatment of POWs—he had learned it in basic training—and he wrongly assumed that if captured the OGs would be treated as POWs. After all, they were in regulation US Army uniforms. They would raise their arms, drop their weapons, and surrender. And up to this point, the OGs had done nothing destructive, had not shot any Germans. Their only offense, a mild one, was that they had landed on enemy territory, and not disguised but in US Army uniforms. However, the grand old American tradition of "never give up the ship" prevailed for numerous years, causing many to criticize Russo's (to them) impotent response to imminent capture. For many, it was not the American way. You stood up and fought back, even if it meant dying. Of course, in the end, no matter the issue of surrender, Vincent Russo and the OGs died for their country.

Franco Lagaxo gave us a picture of what the OGs did after the sun came up on March 23. He saw two uniformed men, armed, walk toward him. They said they were Americans, were in US Army uniforms, and said they wished to speak with him and his mother inside their house. Inside, they stood around the fire; they were still wet after having fallen in the water. They told Lagaxo and his mother that they were looking for a little house (the signal house) near the railroad tracks. Lagaxo said he would take them there.

The group took a path in the woods, and ten minutes later arrived at the little house. Vincent Russo told Lagaxo that this was not the place they sought; this was the southern exit of the tunnel at Bonassola. They wanted the northern entrance, at Framura. After taking some money from Russo, Lagaxo went to town to buy eggs, cheese, and wine, then went home and waited for the OGs; they came back at noon and ate some polenta. Before they left, they told Lagaxo to meet them at 1500 hours at the stable near the house. They all met at the agreed time and walked for an hour until they arrived at a spot where they could see Stazione Framura below. "This is the place where we were supposed to land," one of the Americans said. They sent Lagaxo away and remained there, evaluating the situation.

The next morning two of the OGs were descending the cliff, going down the fissure to the cove, apparently going back to either finish cam-ouflaging the boats or, perhaps, retrieve some items—the remainder of the explosives—they had left behind in their haste. What Lagaxo saw when he got closer was some fishermen gathering items under the direc-tion of Vito Bertone, a local Fascist. The evening before, Gaetano Oneto, a villager, had noticed the bright orange rubber boats poorly camouflaged among the rocks. (Couldn't they have picked a different color? No wonder the boats were spotted.) Oneto went in for a better look. A box in one of the boats had a stencil painted on one side that read "EXPLOSIVE." Lagaxo returned home, and two Americans were standing by the front door; he asked if they had left anything in the boats. They said they had, and Lagaxo told them the Fascists had taken one boat and whatever was inside.

At that moment, the OGs realized they had been discovered; they had to rethink the mission and would eventually have to leave the area. There probably was little hope that they could continue the mission and destroy the tunnels. The OGs returned to the stable.

The poor camouflaging had been their undoing.

His curiosity piqued, Lagaxo took a mule path back to where the boats were. Before he got there, he spotted a group of Fascists and Ger-man soldiers coming toward him. He ran back home and saw several German soldiers and Fascists who had just arrived. They set out searching the area. Two Fascists, Gibatta Bianchi and Bertone, walked to a grove where Lagaxo knew two Americans were hiding.

Bertone spotted them and yelled, "What are you doing here, you ugly pigs?"

"We are Italians," an American replied.

"You are traitors," Bertone said, asking where the other Americans were.

Bertone assumed that because there were three boats, there had to be more than two Americans. A brief exchange of gunfire ensued, and hand grenades were thrown. Vincent Russo was slightly wounded in the face with shrapnel.

At 1030 the Americans surrendered and were disarmed.

Lagaxo saw the Americans coming toward his house with their hands raised; they were immediately surrounded by the Germans and Fascists and locked in the storehouse. The search for more Americans continued until they were satisfied they had caught the whole group.

At 1100 hours, satisfied they had caught all the Americans, the Germans and their Fascist collaborators marched the prisoners to Fascist headquarters in Bonassola, where the prefect, *Commissario* Guglielmini, was the first to interrogate them.

Il Commissario Guglielmini, the prefect of Bonassola, filed an official report concerning what he saw and what happened after the OGs were captured:

> The patrol [involved in the capture] was composed of the following Fascists: Gio Batta Bianchi, Political Secy; Vittorio Bertone, Fascist; Giovanni Ferri, Fascist; Vincenzo Bertini, Station Master, and Luigi Perrone (who later joined of his own volition), Fascists. (The patrol) having learned [about the discovery of the rubber boats] went to the aid of his comrades who had united with a patrol of seven German soldiers located in the [zone on the mountain] indicated by Bertone as the spot where the enemy soldier would probably be found. They initiated an accurate inspection of the zone, roughly from Scalo to Carpenettoia. The Fascist Bertone Vittorio and Ferri Giovanni detached

themselves from the principal group and at about 1015 hours, they discovered two soldiers of enemy nationality who had evidently been placed as sentinels. They caught them by surprise and captured them without the soldier having time to place themselves on guard or alert their companions. But Bertone immediately interrogated one of the two soldiers, seeking to learn if there were others nearby. The interrogated soldiers, who spoke Italian, answered in the negative, stating that the two of them were alone. But Bertone was not convinced inasmuch as he justly surmised that numerous persons and not merely two soldiers must have landed in three rubber boats. He took from his pocket a whistle which he had found in one of the rubber boats and showing it to the captured soldier, said, "Do you want to see how, if I blow this whistle the others will come out?" Bertone then blew the whistle. At the sound, several enemy soldiers who had been hiding in a little vale about a hundred meters [distant] from the place where the first two were captured, jumped to their feet firing their weapons. Fortunately, the [principal] group of Fascists and a German FF.AA. [sic] were only a short distance away in a favorable position. So, making use of hand grenades and small arms, they were able promptly to intervene and surround the enemy who, seeing themselves outnumbered, surrendered time was approximately 1030 hours. During this brief fight the North American Engineer (Lieutenant Russo) was slightly wounded. After being disarmed the enemy soldiers were temporarily located in a stable that was close at hand and were guarded by two Fascists and two Germans while the remainder of the patrol continued to search the entire zone to make sure that there were no other enemy soldier hiding out. After an accurate search the patrol was convinced that there were no other enemy soldiers in the vicinity. The patrol recovered some arms and ammunition found at the place of capture and the enemy soldiers were conducted to Bonassola, where they arrived at about 1200 and were locked in the Fascist headquarters while awaiting orders from qualified higher headquarters. About this time, I [the prefect]

came back from Framura, and having been told of the capture
I went to Fascist headquarters to proceed with an interrogation
of the captured soldiers, who numbered 15, including two officers. The captured soldiers, who were dressed [in khaki-colored
uniforms], turned out to be of North American nationality, the
majority of them being of Italian. Some of them spoke Italian.
From the interrogation of the two officers, I was able to ascertain
that following orders received by them from high headquarter in
Naples they had left Corsica on a [*sic*] PT boat and that when
they neared the Italian coast, they had been transferred to three
rubber boats, also that they landed about 0200 hours on March
22 [*sic*] at the point where the boats were found. Their mission
was to blow up the portion of the railroad from Bonassola to
Framura. Having landed, they went up the mountain and took
lodging in a stable which they found empty and abandoned. They
claimed that they saw Bertone when he passed in front of the
stable in which they were hidden and that had they wanted to,
they could have captured him. I got the impression that they had
no desire to complete the mission which they had been sent and
were content to have been captured. When I asked Lt. Vincent
Russo if he, the son of an Italian, did not feel ashamed to carry
arms against his fatherland, he lowered his head, became red, and
did not answer, but gave me the impression that my words struck
home. At Fascist headquarters the enemy soldiers were searched
by the Germans who found various documents, 30,000 lire, and
some French notes on the prisoners, all of which was consigned
to the German headquarters. German headquarters directed that
the prisoners be sent to Chiaverri [*sic*]. The work of Political secretary Bianchi and of the other Fascists above mentioned was
beyond any eulogy. Their intuitive and courage [deserve] vivid
recognition and I hereby inform the head of the province of their
spirit of sacrifice and their devotion to duty. I attach a list of the
captured North American soldiers. (Signed) The prefect, *Il Commissario* Guglielmini.

According to this report, the OGs were captured by twelve of the enemy: five Italian Fascists and seven German soldiers. In another report, only one German officer and two men made the capture. Lack of clarity here does nothing to evoke an accurate picture of what actually happened.

The Fascist captors had learned much before the Germans arrived, obtaining this information from Lieutenants Traficante and Russo.

After the war ended, statements were obtained from the Fascists. As would be expected, eyewitness reports differ significantly and are often confusing.

Fascist Vittorio Bertone's statement is brief and an example of the confusion surrounding the incident. Some said he was one of the leaders involved in the capture; he was not. While his statement is short, it none-theless provides some fascinating details not found elsewhere:

> I, the undersigned Bertone, Vittorio, residing at Bonassola, hereby declare the following: One day in March 1944, while employed by the Todt Organization, I was sent by the secretary of the Fascio, Bianchi, Giobatta, to see about retrieving a box which had been reported to him the previous evening by Oneto, Gaetano. Oneto accompanied me, and when we arrived at [the cove] we found not only the case, but some rubber rafts. We saw three men fishing from a boat, and with their help we brought the rafts into [shore]. Soon after, a German soldier came down from his OP nearby to see what our activity was all about; when he saw the rafts, he asked us where we got them. Oneto told him that it had been the spot where we found the box, and the German reported the incident to his First Sergeant (who was located in [Bonassola]. The First Sergeant sent eleven men and another Sgt. to investigate, and I went along with them. [Alongside of] the mule path, we found two soldiers in American uniforms—they surrendered without resistance. A Sgt. and a German soldier remained with the two Americans while the other men continued in a search for more. They found thirteen others—also in American uniform. /s/ Bertone, Vittorio.

Fascist Vincenzo di Pietro Bertini's statement also gives us many details not found in the others':

> In reference to the incident about which the Prefect of Bonassola wrote regarding the capture of fifteen American soldiers, Bertini swears as follows: On March 24 1944 at about 0900 hours, I heard rumors that some Americans had landed. It was said that a certain Oneto Gaetano, mason, had found a box on which was written ["munition," "explosives,"] in a strange language. Coming to Bonassola he informed the secretary of the Fascist party, Bianchi, G. B., of his discovery. Bianchi then sent Bertone and Oneto to cover the case of explosive but it was no longer there. Instead of finding the box, they found rubber boats hidden among the rocks. These boats were brought to Bonosola [*sic*] later. Bianchi alerted the German garrison and six Germans along with Bianchi, Ferri, and Berton Vittorio set out. The distance from [Bonassola] to the point where the boats were located was about 800 air line meters. I was located in the general vicinity. I met two Germans of this patrol, who invited me to go with them. However, I lagged behind, and when I arrived, the Americans [had already surrendered and were captives]. They held their hands on their heads. Going back to Fascist headquarters, I remained about a hundred meters behind Perrone Luigi. At Fascist headquarters the prisoners said they were hungry. I was present and talked with almost all the prisoners because they talked Italian. I asked who the officer was, and they showed me an insignia which he had under his collar. I went to the Commissioner to get something for them to eat but he shouted that he would give them nothing. In the meantime, he continued to interrogate the officers. I procured water and aspirin for one of the prisoners. Upon my insistence, they were finally given bread. This was about 1300 hours. Then I went to eat at home. When I returned for the second time to give the prisoners bread, I heard the Commissioner, Guglielmone, say to Lt. Vincent Russo, "Aren't you the son of Italians, ashamed to fight against your brothers?" The Lt. did not answer.

The Commissioner asked how long they had been there. He (Russo?) answered: two days. "We disembarked from a PT boat about two miles off the coast about 2300 hours, and we landed on shore about midnight." The Commissioner asked why they had remained there for two days and what they had done. I heard the Lt. answer, "We have not yet located the actual place for our mission." Some people said that the Americans were to have blown the tunnel from Framura to [Bonassola]. After this I was through but returned about 1530 hours to give Lt. Russo some bread. At that time, a German truck with about ten men arrived. The Germans cleared the place where the prisoners were and went in. The Fascist Commissioner and the Secretary remained. About 1700 hours the American prisoners were put on the truck and taken toward La Spezia. After the departure of the prisoners, I did not speak of the incident with anyone, and I heard no further information about them. Commissioner Guglielmone made a report against me to the Prefect and the Federal Secretary because I did not want to assume responsibility as Fascist Political Secretary. (signed) Bertini, Vincenzo, Genoa, 1 May 1945.

The OSS, still hanging onto a sliver of hope that the OGs were alive and hiding out somewhere, believed for the briefest of moments that they could have been on their way or, perhaps, had already arrived at the pre-designated safe house in Babio, in accordance with their contingency plan.

Then news arrived in Bastia that reduced this hope to almost zero.

On March 27, the Wehrmacht transmitted an ominous communiqué at 1500 hours (GMT time) via Berlin that was monitored by the BBC; it was broadcast in German and then English:

The Supreme Command of the Armed Forces announces: On the East Coast of the Gulf of Genoa, a party of US Commandos consisting of two officers and thirteen men, which landed north-west of Spezia, was wiped out.

Attached was a duplicate version that aired from Rome on March 28 at 2300 hours, a couple of days after the OGs had been murdered by firing squad. The communiqué deliberately used the term *ausgelöscht* ("wiped out") when what they meant was "executed," which had occurred on the morning of March 26. And by that time the OGs were, indeed, all dead and buried and in a common grave.

The OSS had good reason to doubt this report, perhaps believing it was disinformation by the Germans. At the time, OSS had no way to validate the report, mainly the worth or meaning of "wiped out." They felt helpless.

The disposition of the OGs after they landed was becoming more apparent: They had come ashore around midnight (22/23 March) at a cove in their orange rubber boats below Carpeneggio, La Spezia province. (Bonassola, Carpeneggio, and La Spezia are interchangeable as the pinpoints where the OGs landed because the towns are so close to one another; they are all in La Spezia province.) As soon as they arrived, they hastily attempted to camouflage the orange dinghies before they ascended a fissure at the 150-meter mountain—this camouflaging was done hastily and ineffectively. A fisherman could see the dinghies from his fishing boat and he reported what he saw.

Meanwhile, the OSS pressed on, desperate to find their brother commandos and determine whether the "wiped out" report was accurate or they had misinterpreted the German version of the communiqué.

Another eyewitness to the events after the Ginny OGs arrived at Carpeneggio, Angelonia Viviani, who lived on the mountaintop near Carpeneggio, added some rich details:

> On the morning of March 24, 1944, at about 0915 hours, I saw that from my stable . . . some smoke arising, and I neared it to see what was happening. At about 15 meters from [my] stable, I heard myself called by a soldier whom I later learned to be an American officer . . . called me closer. When I was near him, he inquired of me if many armed Germans or Fascists were at the "Salto dell Lepre" battery. To this . . . I responded that there were 3 or 4 Germans . . . but some 15 Fascists, after which they

courteously asked me if I could furnish them with some food. I agreed, [saying] that I would bring him [*sic*] the said food at 1600 hours of the same day. After this, the officer returned into my stable where, I presume, they warmed themselves and dried their clothes because from what I had seen they were very wet, and I went back to getting some greens. About 15 minutes later, I heard an explosion of a hand grenade. I learned later that said hand grenade was thrown by Bianchi against two American soldiers who were acting as sentinels about 100 meters from the stable. Eight of the two were wounded and were therefore captured and taken to the site near the stable. Shortly thereafter, the Germans descended, and I saw an American officer fire a burst against a German who was nearing the stable. Contemporary [?] those remaining in the stable gave themselves up, [were] made to come out, [and] were taken to the site where [the Fascists] Bertini, Ferri, Perrone, Bianchi, and Bertone, were very elated and Perone also stated the following, "I am going to see those 'cowardly' Americans to spit on their faces." Interrogated at the spot by a German, who accused me of having brought something to eat to the Americans; the same stated that I [would be punished]. After this interrogation, I returned home, where I arrived at about 1000 hours. Other than this I have nothing to add.

CHAPTER 4

The Pistol on the Door Handle

ON THE AFTERNOON OF MARCH 24, THE CAPTURED OGs WERE TRUCKED to Bonassola, a commune in the province of La Spezia in the region of Liguria, located about sixty kilometers southeast of Genoa and about twenty kilometers northwest of La Spezia, the second-largest city in the Ligurian region after Genoa. There, they were ordered out of the trucks, placed in different trucks, and transported to *Oberst* (Colonel) Kurt Almer's Brigade Almers, located in a small castle at Carozzo on a hillside three or four kilometers north of La Spezia. (A brigade is usually composed of three to six battalions, three thousand to five thousand soldiers, and can be commanded by a general officer or, in this case, a colonel [*oberst*]).

There are no comments, statements, or other forms of communication on record from the OGs. However, the US Army made a film and took photographs of General Dostler's trial and subsequent execution. Most of the details concerning what occurred were gleaned from reports and eyewitness testimonies made after the war. At Carozzo, German counterintelligence (*Abwehr*) officers immediately began intense interrogations, both by the German Navy (*Kriegsmarine*) and the Wehrmacht.

The first German officer to start the interrogations was *Oberleutnant* (1st Lieutenant) Wolfgang Körbitz, Brigade Almers's intelligence officer—this at around 1800 hours. Körbitz dealt with anti-partisan and intelligence issues. During a meeting with Guglielmini in La Spezia on March 24, he learned about the capture of the OGs. He immediately left the meeting and headed to brigade headquarters at the castle in Carozzo, arriving there around 1830 hours, and saw the Americans. They were dressed in their US Army regulation field uniforms. Körbitz asked an orderly to get food and water and have them sent to the building that would serve as a prison. Once there, Hans Bertram Baumgarten, the officer in charge of the prison, searched them for identification, weapons, and personal items. He discovered four wristwatches, multiple nail files, and almost thirty thousand lire. Then he put Traficante and Russo in separate cells and the rest of the OGs in three other cells.

The interrogation quickly fizzled; it became apparent that Körbitz's English was insufficient to push him through interrogating the English-speaking OGs effectively. A call was put through to La Spezia for *Kriegsmarine Korvettenkapitän* (Captain) Friedrich Klaps, chief of the Counterintelligence Station, head of the German Navy Intelligence office at La Spezia. Klaps was ordered to Brigade Almers headquarters to take over interrogating the OGs. When Klaps arrived, he was more interested in obtaining tactical naval information regarding Allied intentions for invading the Ligurian coast. And because Klaps could only speak and understand about 75 percent of the Americans' English, he summoned another *Kriegsmarine* officer he thought perfect for the interrogations, *Oberleutnant zur See* (Lieutenant) Georg Sessler, his Abwehr assistant, an intelligence officer with a curious background.

Before the war, Sessler had worked on the docks in New York City, and he spoke fluent American English with an American accent. Finally, the Germans had found an officer who spoke "excellent English." Sessler took on all subsequent Ginny OG interrogations and would soon be deeply involved in trying to either save their lives or at least suspend their execution. Thus he was an essential witness to the Ginny OG situation and its maneuverings. (Sessler surrendered at the end of the war to Americans in Milan on May 4, 1945. Between May 11 and May 13, he was interrogated extensively at the Combined Service Detailed Interrogation Center in Florence, where his involvement in Ginny was vigorously probed.)

In the summer of 1945, Georg Sessler added pertinent details from the military perspective concerning the capture of the Ginny OGs:

Near the landing site was located a small fishing village in which there was a station of Fascist shore police. No one had heard of the landing nor of the subsequent movements of the group. [Sessler], however, was told by German Army officers[,] that a fishing boat returning to the village about 0800 hours had reported sighting rubber boats among the rocks near the shoreline. According to [Sessler] the camouflage had been effective only from the land side, that is, from the beach, from the railway embankment, and from the hillside. From the seaside, however, portions of the boats were visible. Following the report to the Fascists shore patrol, a search had been instituted. The three boats were found, as well as two cases of explosives, and it was concluded that from the nature of the concealment that those who had landed were planning to return and therefore were probably in the area. The whole zone behind the landing point had been evacuated of civilian inhabitants[,] and therefore, a systematic search was instituted of the whole hillside area. In one house on the hillside, the men were discovered by a patrol of 3 or 4 Fascist shore police who covered the group with automatic rifles while they sent one of their members to the village for aid. The circumstances leading to capture were as follows according to [Sessler's informant]: The house in which the group was located was approached by two paths, one leading to the front door and the other to the rear door, both paths continuing beyond the hours toward the fishing village. The [OG sentry] was stationed at the front entrance at a point where he commanded the approach from the village along both paths. He did not, however, command the approach [to the rear of the house by the path leading to the cove]. Therefore, when the patrol approached by the path leading [from the cover], a complete surprise was effected and the men were discovered, as much to their surprise as to themselves, while [the Americans] were resting or sleeping. It was not possible [for them] to make any resistance whatsoever. With the arrival of the Fascist reinforcements from the village, the men were brought into the La Spezia area in the afternoon and turned over to the German Army Commandant of the La Spezia area, Col. Almers, who evidently immediately informed his general headquarters. Enlisted men were divided among three rooms in the cellar of Almer's castle and the two officers were placed together at the first room. [Sessler] insists that he was not able to learn any more than has been indicated above from Russo[,] and that neither Russo nor from any other of the other men could be ascertained what organization had dispatched them beyond the Pioneer Company, the number of which has been forgotten.

Klaps stated that the enlisted OGs "did very little talking," something that all soldiers are taught in basic training—name, rank, and serial number; that's it. He learned "some information about shipping in the Bastia Harbor." The OGs, he stated, were interrogated "with regard to divisional signs of units on Corsica also concerning the presence of aviation units on the island." While some of this was useful, it was not what they were after—which was the purpose of the Ginny OGs' mission, the target(s), and so on. Klaps remembered, too, that all the German officers involved in the interrogations "believed that the [Ginny OGs] to be regular commandos, and himself and Sessler thought this until further interrogation indicated otherwise."

Then Sessler and Klaps started thinking about the treatment of the OGs. A bit of humanity was creeping into the cold, hard reality of soldiering and killing. While this mild debate ensued, each was mindful of the consequences that would follow if their superiors discovered that they were showing sympathy toward these Americans. Unlike others in the command, Klaps, Körbitz, and Sessler were not hard-core Nazis.

Klaps expressed one side of the argument: "According to a Füehrer Order then in force, members of 'so-called Commandos,' either in uniform or in civilian clothes, were to be eliminated." This seemed clear.

Sessler and Körbitz agreed. Details of the interrogation had indicated that the men were not members of "so-called Commandos" and, therefore, were to be treated as POWs. Saying that, because of his low rank, Körbitz refused to take forward any recommendation for leniency. According to Klaps, officers in the intelligence community were very excited about the possibility of a landing on other sections of the Ligurian coast.

In a veiled attempt to save the lives of the OGs, Klaps then sent a telex, his second, to 75th Army Corps stating that if harm came to the OGs there could be a good chance of reprisals against German prisoners and that everyone in La Spezia knew of the case.

It was probably here, when the interrogations began, that Klaps and Sessler started to feel a spark of sympathy for the OGs. They were, after all, "brothers in arms," and more than likely the first time they had come face-to-face with the so-called enemy: American soldiers. Like them, they fought for their country and were prepared to die for what they believed. They were not monsters; they hadn't harmed anyone or destroyed any property. Face-to-face, looking one another in the eyes, had a much more human dimension: These were human beings, much like themselves in many ways, and there was a good chance they could all be dead in a few days. Except for their uniforms and languages, there wasn't much difference between the Americans and the Germans. The interrogators were putting themselves into the shoes of the OGs. They were white, about the same ages. Like Sessler, Klaps, and Körbitz, they had parents, brothers and sisters, girlfriends. Unlike the officers at headquarters, who had never seen these men in person, it was not easy for the three to pass judgment, to order an execution. The Germans were starting to show signs of empathy and, in the process, beginning to risk their own lives and careers.

After Lieutenant Russo's interrogation, Sessler took on No. 3 and No. 4—this was how the prisoners were referred to, by numbers. Unlike Russo, No. 3 and No. 4 refused to cooperate with Sessler beyond name, rank, and serial number.

On March 24, Headquarters, LXXV Army Corps, was informed of the capture. A short time later, headquarters looked for any tactical information, if any had arrived. Headquarters was still concerned about any possible "invasions" of the coastline, even more concerned about that than possible attacks on targets the OGs might have had in mind—particularly on landing in Liguria from Corsica. Sessler reassured headquarters that there was no evidence of that.

At 2200 hours, he asked Klaps to telex his overall impressions to headquarters and urged a delay in the executions.

At 0030 hours, Klaps's report was complete and dispatched to higher headquarters.

At 0130 hours, summaries were telexed to *Generalfeldmarshall* (General Field Marshal) Kesselring's headquarters on Monte Soratte (which he would later deny). Copies went to Klaps's superior, Col. Otto Helffrich, Chief (*Leiter*) of Military Intelligence Station Italy (Abwehr-stelle Italien).

⸺

With the Ginny OGs at Carozzo, Sessler's questioning commenced at around 1800 hours on March 24 and continued through the night until 0400–0500 hours the following day. Klaps, Körbitz, and several other officers were present when Sessler interrogated the first OG, 1st Lt. Paul Traficante, C/O of the mission. Traficante and his party were assigned to handle security throughout the mission, particularly at the tunnels' entrances, looking for German or Italian forces.

Traficante stood fast. He had completed one Army draft assignment but had reenlisted after hearing the news of Pearl Harbor while at his brother's wedding. Sessler could not pry anything more substantive from him than name, rank, and serial number, the only information American soldiers are taught to provide the enemy when in captivity. The two Ginny OG enlisted men who followed Traficante also did not offer anything substantive for the increasingly frustrated German intelligence officers; they had been at it for nearly two tedious hours and gotten almost nowhere.

Next, the interrogators started probing Lt. Vincent J. Russo, overall commanding officer of the shore party. Russo, born in Montclair, New Jersey, on March 27, 1917, and raised there, had been a construction worker before the war. At his capture and execution, he was twenty-seven years old.

During the interrogation of Traficante and the two enlisted men, Russo had been isolated from the other OGs. Before escorting him into the interrogation room, Sessler decided to try a "stock interrogator's ruse" on Russo suggested by Klaps. Sessler described this ruse in a pretrial statement to Maj. Frederick W. Roche, the judge advocate/prosecutor at the Dostler trial; after the war, Roche elicited the "ruse" details from Sessler:

Major Roche: Will you tell the commission briefly how Lieutenant Russo came to tell you the story of his mission?

Sessler: After I interrogated Lieutenant Traficante and the two enlisted men, I was still on the beginning point. I didn't find out anything at all, so by this time all I knew was this: that those men were found on the beach, and I figured out that they must have come out in some boats, of course, and when Lt. Russo came [into the room] I told him that we had got a so-called *Führerbefehl*, a leader order from Hitler, and this here *Führerbefehl* says that saboteurs and members of a crew of a commando raiding team have to be shot by *Führerbefehl* order. I told [Lieutenant Russo I had] told Lieutenant Traficante the same thing, and then I told him that because of this Lt. Traficante made a full statement of his mission; and to begin with I said, "I know that you left Bastia and first I want to know about what time." I didn't know that they came from Bastia, but I figured it out because it was the shortest distance from that place where they landed, so Lt. Russo told me they left Bastia by this and this time. I don't remember exactly when it was. I had a couple of papers on my desk, and I told him that it does not agree with the statement from Lieutenant Traficante. I told him Lieutenant Traficante gave me a different time about a half an hour earlier or later, and he said, well, the time he gave me is the time, the only time he remembers exactly. So, I told him to continue. Then he told me that they left in two American patrol boats and following that he told me the story of the mission.

Major Roche: He told you the story of the mission that you have already related?

Sessler: Yes, that is right.

Major Roche: To sum up then, you tricked Russo into telling you what happened?

Sessler: Yes, sir.

By midnight, the Germans had learned much about the OGs' mission: They knew their unit in Bastia, what the mission was, and much more.

The unit that kept records of the Ginny OGs was Brigade Almers—named for its commanding officer, *Oberst* (Colonel) Kurt Almers. This unit was subordinate to the 75th Army Corps, whose commander was Lt. Gen. (*General der Infanterie*) Anton Dostler.

Dostler joined the German army in 1910 and served as a junior officer during World War I. From the start of World War II to 1940, he served as chief of staff of the Seventh Army. He went on to command the 57th Infantry Division for one year, the 163rd Infantry Division in 1942 and, after some temporary stand-ins at Corps, was appointed commander of the 75th Army Corps in Italy from January to July 1944. After this, he was commander of the Venetian Coast until the war ended. He had received numerous awards and decorations but was never awarded the Knight's Cross, which bothered him.

Around 2100 hours on March 24, Klaps told Sessler that he believed Hitler's Commando Order applied to the prisoners and that the Ginny OGs would be shot at 0500 hours on March 25.

The next morning at 0400 hours, a German infantry captain arrived at Carozzo and ordered the Ginny OGs to be executed according to an order he had received. Sessler showed the captain a telex he had sent requesting a postponement. The captain was confused and asked Sessler for advice; Sessler told him to wait before doing anything further.

At this point, after much questioning of the Ginny OGs, Sessler equivocated—he was uncertain whether the OGs were commandos or soldiers on a military mission (as several others believed). If they were soldiers, they should not be executed. But who could say with certainty—although they dressed like regular soldiers, they did not carry identification attesting to one category or the other.

Sessler then resumed his interrogation but got nothing more than name, rank, and serial number. He even tried the same ruse, but it went nowhere.

Based on the information Klaps had gained so far, he prepared a report for General Dostler. It stated that the Americans had come to the Ligurian coast aboard two US Navy gunboats. They were indeed American soldiers dressed in regulation US Army uniforms carrying US weapons. Their purpose was to blow up the two tunnels at Bonassola near Stazione

Framura. Further, he wrote, they were based in Corsica, commanded by a Colonel Livermore. He believed their regimental headquarters was in North Africa but was not sure. At 0200 the report was dispatched via teletype to 75th Army Corps headquarters, arriving at 0215 hours.

At 0400 hours Sessler and Klaps went to their rooms to freshen up. They would be back soon.

When Sessler and Klaps arrived later that morning, an official from the *Sicherheitsdienst* was waiting to take part in the interrogations. His presence was ominous. The *Sicherheitsdienst des Reichsführers–SS* (Security Service of the Reichsführer-SS), or SD, was the intelligence agency of the SS and the Nazi Party. They had a menacing and intimidating presence wherever they were, which they of course relished and played on entirely. According to Hitler's Commando Order, it would be the SD that would take captured commandos or saboteurs away, never to be seen again. The SD officer was there to take the Ginny OGs if he thought it necessary. The interrogations went on, but the SD man did not feel it appropriate to take part in them himself. He seemed pleased with how the interrogations were proceeding. But before he left, the SD officer asked Klaps if he would be allowed to join the questioning. Yes, was the response. The Americans gave the same nonanswers to the SD man as they had to the others: name, rank, serial number. Then, probably in a show of defiance, they stopped giving even that information and would not provide their home addresses in the United States.

Then, at around 1030 hours, March 25, Klaps received a portentous telegram from General Dostler:

The captured Americans are to be shot immediately. Dostler.

On March 25, in the afternoon, Brigade Commander Colonel Almers, Klaps, and Sessler discussed the status of the Ginny OGs in terms of how they should be treated. They were thinking in terms of the *Führer befehl* then in force. This was the start of equivocation, confusion, and soul-searching.

Sessler then urged Klaps to telex his impression to a higher authority and get a definitive answer. At the same time, he asked Klaps, at the very least, to try to delay the executions while he continued the interrogations.

The next morning the prisoners were brought to a nearby barn, and Sessler began the second day's interrogation of prisoners No. 5 and No. 6. It was the same runaround; they gave Sessler no new information about their reason for being in enemy territory. From their demeanor, Sessler now believed that all the prisoners were sure they would be executed by firing squad as soon as possible. No. 8 said, "Here's mud in your eye"— in other words, proposing a "toast" for his upcoming execution. Then an astonishing coincidence took place:

In the 1930s Sessler had worked at the Hamburg-American Line for two years on the docks in Hoboken, New Jersey. At the same time, he was a spy for the Abwehr, using the undercover name of George Sinclair. Both Sessler and No. 8, who turned out to be Joseph Farrell, recalled that they had met in New York City and had frequently seen each other working on the docks as longshoremen. Sessler later recalled that this prisoner's name was Joe, of Jewish extraction. When Farrell told Klaps he recognized him, they couldn't believe it. Farrell had been an ice delivery boy at the Hamburg-American Line in 1936–1937, bringing ice to Piers 84 and 86, where the German liners docked. The conversation became friendlier and more personal as Farrell talked about his family life. Then Farrell told Klaps that he and the other OGs were sure they soon would be in front of a firing squad, that it was over for them.

"My superiors and I," Klaps said, "are doing everything we can to have you evacuated to a POW camp." Farrell was then dismissed, and Klaps interviewed the others until 2000 hours.

In *Last Hero: Wild Bill Donovan*, Anthony Cave Brown wrote that Sessler had "connections with the British Intelligence" in 1944, but Brown does not cite his source for this interesting tidbit. However, while working for the Hamburg–North American Lines in the 1930s, using George Sinclair as a cover, Sessler had been an Abwehr spy in the USA and Allied intelligence. And now, in March 1944, he was an intelligence officer in the German army interrogating the Ginny OGs in what would be a historic mission. Quite an incredible coincidence—one of the many in Operation Ginny—because Sessler showed sympathy for a man who was about to stand in front of a firing squad. He was doing as much as he could without jeopardizing both his career and his life to save the Ginny OGs.

At Brigade Almers headquarters, the day was filled with confusion, indecision, and, yes, sympathy—no one knew what to do with the fifteen Ginny OGs. Several of the men—Klaps, Sessler, and Körbitz, in particular—knew in their hearts that the *Führerbefehl* could be viewed as criminal, draconian, and vengeful. There were two viewpoints: Send them to POW camps or, since they were spies, have them shot according to Hitler's Commando Order. It was clear what that order said, and to disobey it would lead to a court-martial.

Klaps called for a conference with Sessler, Körbitz, and the SD officer. He went around the table and asked everyone if he thought the Americans were spies, members of a commando group, or soldiers. The consensus was that the Americans were not members of a commando force. Based on this consensus, Klaps advised Körbitz to report to his superiors, summarizing their meeting and rendering the opinion that it would be a severe mistake to execute the Americans.

Klaps sent his report to Colonel Almers via telex, asking that the execution be halted or postponed for further analysis and discussion. The note went to *Oberst* (Colonel) Horst Kraehe, General Dostler's chief of staff. After receiving the telex, Almers called Colonel Kraehe to be sure he had received Körbitz's telex. Listening in on the other end of the line was General Dostler, who interrupted the conversation.

"Almers," Dostler said in a less than friendly voice, "listen to me. We cannot change anything. You know the *Führerbefehl*. The execution is to be carried out. You know that the *Führerbefehl* contains a clause according to which officers who do not execute the order are to be tried by court-martial." A few more arguments were put forward to Dostler, but they made no difference. Dostler hung up. Kraehe, however, was still on the line, and Klaps made a fruitless attempt to get either a postponement or a withdrawal of the order. Kraehe told him the order would be carried out and it was so stated in a statement Dostler made at 2400 hours. Nevertheless, Klaps asked Kraehe to do his best to postpone further discussion.

At 0700 hours the following day, Klaps called Kraehe and spoke to Dostler. Because of security regulations, their conversation was "camouflaged," or "veiled."

Klaps referred to the Ginny OGs as "guests," saying, "They were not as bad men as we thought [at] first but harmless people"; that they were not "saboteurs" or "commandos." He then added that the executions should be delayed for further review. Besides, Klaps added, "We should interrogate them further from the point of view of the [tactical aspect], and we have to find out further whether if there is any connection with the Italian civilian population or Italian Partisans, because it could have been a commando or so-called commando." Klaps added a menacing point that he thought might help sway Dostler to rescind or delay the executions: The executions could result in repercussions by the Americans against German prisoners of war; he was referring to reprisals.

Dostler replied that he had heard things differently, that he had received other reports. Now the conversation descended into a shouting match. Dostler stated that he was furious at the whole matter, and he, Dostler, a "General of the Infantry," threatened "to break Klaps" because he was now interfering with the *Führerbefehl* and the whole convoluted situation. "Now," Dostler said, "put your thoughts together and send them to me in telex immediately. And," he added, "I want this interrogation concluded by 0700 hours tomorrow morning."

Dostler hung up, but before he did he said, "I want you to carry out my orders, do you understand me? And this you must confirm your compliance via the telex. This order is now on its way to *Oberst* Almers."

Klaps was ordered to send Dostler a telex outlining the points they had just made on the phone; Dostler added that he could not speak freely on the telephone about the matter for security reasons.

Dostler, with the telephone operator acting as a go-between, asked Klaps how much time he would need to conclude the interrogations. Klaps replied, "five minutes" or "one week," depending on how much the prisoners "talk."

And that was the end of the conversation. Klaps hung up the phone and set out to compose a telex:

Please postpone execution of *Führerbefehl* because it has not been established whether the fifteen Americans belong to Commandos or whether they are cases coming under *Führerbefehl* at all. There is a possibility for repercussions against German prisoners of war. Further interrogations necessary. It should be determined whether there are threads leading from the Americans to Italian civilian population or Partisans.

Oberst Almers and his staff officers were reluctant to carry out the executions. Despite their efforts to rescind or postpone the order, they felt that any further resistance would be futile.

Showing how concerned he had been about saving the OGs' lives, after the war Sessler related an incident he thought would give the OGs a chance to escape.

He had Joseph Farrell brought back to the interrogation room. When he sat down, Sessler told him he had bad news, that he and several other German officers had done everything they could to change the order, but now there was no chance. After a short conversation about families, Sessler offered to do anything he could to help Farrell's family. Sessler was emotionally moved by the way Farrell took the news of his impending death. Sessler then offered him a chance—a risky one—to escape and possibly help his men escape at the same time. Sessler told Farrell that his pistol was in his holster, attached to a belt hanging on the doorknob of the door leading from the interrogation room. If he pressed down on the doorknob, the pistol would fall out of the holster. "Take it on your way out of the room," Sessler said. "Then head for the mountains—that's where the Partisans are."

At first, Farrell refused. It took him a couple of minutes to come around to the notion, surmising that it would be better to at least try to escape rather than do nothing and be executed. As Farrell went through the door, he pressed down on the handle and the pistol fell to the floor. Sessler, meanwhile, distracted Sergeant Neubauer, who did not notice the gun's absence. This was the last time Sessler saw Joseph Farrell.

Apparently, after he had the pistol, Farrell passed it on to Lieutenant Traficante. In Sessler's words, this is what occurred after Farrell left the interrogation room and was on his way to the execution site:

[Sessler's] gun was found on the person of Lt. Traficante while the whole group was being conducted to the place of execution. The circumstances, [Sessler] learned later, were that following the [loading] of the Americans into the truck in which they sat on two benches facing each, the [American] Infantry Lt. [probably Traficante, CO of the security party] attempted to draw the gun out of the pocket of his sheepskin jacket. The movement was noted by the guard sitting opposite him, who covered him immediately. There was no shooting, but the whole group was again searched for weapons and then taken to the place of execution. [Sessler] believes that when No. 8 left the interrogation room, he returned to the stalls and turned the pistol over to Traficante and that it had then [been] decided that the final attempt would be made when the whole group had been put on a truck.

On the morning of the same day, [Sessler] was called for interrogation at Almers's headquarters by the Ic 1st Lt. [Schultz] with regard to the pistol that had been found on Traficante. [Sessler] admitted that the pistol and belt were hanging on the door and therefore easily procurable under the circumstance. [Sessler] could not, however, explain to the satisfaction of the Ic officer why he had not noticed when he replaced his pistol belt on his body that there was no weight of the pistol in the holster. For 13 days thereafter, [Sessler] was called to Almers's headquarters and interrogated with regard to what was considered a breach of conduct on his part.

What Traficante intended once he had the pistol in hand from Farrell and aboard the truck is speculation. At the very least, Traficante would make an attempt to free the whole group, possibly take over the truck and the Germans' weapons—maybe take one as a hostage—and then go from there, improvising the entire way. They certainly would not have gotten far; the area was filled with Fascists and German troops, and their escape would have been immediately broadcast throughout the area. But a bad plan is always better than no plan at all. Perhaps they would have made a dash for the coast and the rubber dinghies. Whatever the intent, it will never be known—except that the notion of escape was better than remaining passive and simply waiting to be lined up for execution.

What is known is that Farrell returned to the stalls with Klaps's pistol under his jacket and gave the pistol to Lieutenant Traficante. At this point, it is safe to surmise that the group would try to escape either on the way to the trucks or once inside, where they stood a chance to overcome the guards. When they arrived at the trucks, Traficante went for the pistol; it got stuck on his jacket and a guard saw him struggling to get the pistol out. A scuffle occurred. Traficante, Alfred De Flumeri, and Farrell attempted to get the pistol, but failed.

Sessler's account of what happened in the truck can be construed as self-serving, viewed as an effort to gain leniency for himself from the Americans at war's end if captured. As an intelligence officer with experience overseas, he had to be cunning and ingenuous. Indeed, Sessler saw the war ending soon in favor of the Allies. He knew that if captured and found to be involved in the deaths of the OGs, he would be classified as a war criminal and tried. But later, independently of Sessler, Klaps confirmed Sessler's rendering of his "pistol" story and his attempt to help Farrell. Whatever Sessler's motive was, he tried to effect an escape for the OGs and should not be forgotten for the effort.

From there through the execution of the fifteen Ginny OGs, the question of execution evolved into a hazardous undertaking for several German officers—not least being Sessler. Many on both Almers's and Dostler's staffs did not believe the OGs deserved to face a firing squad; these officers were trying to do the decent thing and save the Ginny OGs from Hitler's vengeance and hatred. Even speaking about their positions regarding sparing the OGs could have been seen as an act of treason.

A confrontation of wills and morality soon evolved, with those in favor of executing the prisoners and those against it for legal and moral reasons. And then there was the matter of obeying illegal orders. Several officers—Sessler in particular—were placing their lives on the line by trying to save the American OGs. Allowing his pistol to possibly be obtained by a POW would surely be a significant offense in the German army, one undoubtedly punishable by death—by firing squad at that.

On March 25, around noon, Sessler met with Körbitz, telling him that he had received a telex around 0900–0930 hours that morning from 75th Army Corps Headquarters addressed to *Oberst* (Colonel) Almers, ordering him that "the captured Americans are to be shot immediately [signed] Dostler." Almers read the order, and Körbitz told Sessler that he overheard Almers tell Klaps that he, too, had misgivings about applying Hitler's draconian Commando Order.

Almers said, "I don't think this order is that the execution should be in the next half hour, but I will try to delay it while I get in touch with Headquarters LXXV Army Corps again."

Almers—a brigade commander, a colonel, a high-ranking officer certainly familiar with the *Führerbefehl*—was starting to see that, perhaps, an illegal order had been passed down from *General der Infantrie* Dostler—an order that, perhaps, Almers could not morally obey.

Several other officers tacitly agreed. Such thinking, if made public, would certainly put their careers, even their lives, at stake, potentially resulting in courts-martial, imprisonment, and execution. They all knew they could only go so far—that if they went too far and disobeyed Dostler's order to execute, they themselves would be executed. If everyone in the German army did that, there'd be no one left in the ranks.

Earlier, everyone at Brigade Almers headquarters involved in the case had been sure that the Ginny OGs were "regular commandos." And because of the interrogations, Sessler, Klaps, and Körbitz were starting to believe that the prisoners did not fit the criteria specified in the Commando Order.

Orders or not, the matter was perplexing for all involved. None wanted to take a fall for Dostler or anyone else—in other words, no one wanted to face possible court-martial for the sake of saving anyone's reputation. As the minutes and hours moved forward, some German officers were having misgivings about executing men whose only crime had been landing on enemy soil.

Undeniably, as military men, they felt that a serious attempt should be made to rescind, or at least postpone, the executions and give the matter much more thought before taking the lives of fifteen men. Time was running out for the OGs huddled in the nearby barn awaiting their fate. When they set out on the mission, they had to have initially thought that if they got captured, the Germans would treat them as POWs—a situation that was now dissolving into something much more ominous.

Despite saying he would call headquarters, Almers did not convince Klaps that he would intervene at that time. According to Körbitz, at some point that afternoon, Almers telephoned the 75th Army Corps, thinking he would speak with Dostler. However, Körbitz spoke with Dostler's (GSO) chief of staff, *Oberst* (Colonel) Kraehe. This would indicate that at this point, Almers was not confident that the execution order stood a chance of being rescinded.

Klaps, still confident that he, as well as Körbitz and Sessler, believed a stay of execution was appropriate, again called the 75th Army Corps to try to convince Dostler that the matter needed further investigation and the executions should be postponed. Klaps felt that since he was an integral part of the interrogation process, he could speak directly with Dostler again, an officer with the authority to rescind the order to execute.

Chapter 5

General Dostler Rescinds

By midnight, March 24/25, Field Marshal Kesselring's headquarters at Monte Soratte, forty-five kilometers north of Rome, had been notified of the capture of the Ginny fifteen.

At his trial after the war, Kesselring and his immediate staff committed perjury, claiming that his headquarters had never received this information and he had not ordered or tacitly agreed to the execution of the Ginny OGs. In fact, he claimed (falsely) that he wasn't even at his Monte Soratte headquarters at the time.

On the same date, March 25, Dostler rescinded his execution order, which surprised everyone—but not for the reason one might assume. He was waiting for approval from the next higher echelon, Army Group von Zangen (*Armee-Gruppe von Zangen*), named for its commander, *Generalleutnant* (Lieutenant General) Gustav-Adolf von Zangen, Dostler's immediate commander. Von Zangen, recipient of Germany's esteemed Knight's Cross of the Iron Cross with Oak Leaves, was an officer that many thought would change Dostler's mind in favor of the OGs.

That afternoon, Dostler told Klaps that he had until 0700 hours the next day, March 26, to execute the OGs. However, the order had not yet been put in writing for approvals, which bought the OGs some time.

Klaps was now even more committed to preventing the executions. But late afternoon on March 25, he received another telex at Brigade Almers that was initiated at the 75th Army Corps: "The executions will be carried out by 0700 hours, March 26." With the telex in hand, Dostler now felt that the order to execute had been blessed "by higher headquarters" and that he could proceed officially.

Back at Brigade Almers, Körbitz started typing what Klaps dictated, composing the telex demanded by General Dostler. Two copies were dispatched by 2000 hours, March 26: One was addressed to Headquarters, 75th Army Corps; a second went to Monte Soratte, headquarters of Gen. Rudolf Toussaint, plenipotentiary general in occupied Italy. About an hour later, the dispatcher at Brigade Almers reported to Klaps that both telexes had been sent and gave him the arrival times.

Klaps returned to his quarters sometime after midnight, March 26, feeling anxious and frustrated. He called Dostler's headquarters and attempted to speak with the duty officer, the intelligence officer, the operations officer, and the chief of general staff—everyone except the cook. He wanted to know if General Dostler had received the telex Dostler had asked for—but none knew if the telex had been shown to Dostler.

Klaps persevered. At 0430 he finally got Dostler out of bed and on the phone.

It is unknown if Klaps, a commander in *Kriegsmarine* intelligence, believed he was overstepping his authority, even jeopardizing himself, by doing what he perceived as a naval intelligence officer doing due diligence in an urgent matter. He believed that his rank, position, and the severe issue he was calling about justified calling and waking a general of the infantry.

The connection with General Dostler was so poor that the telephone operator had to intervene, passing along their conversations to the other. Speaking in "camouflage" again, Dostler informed Klaps that the executions should be scheduled. Klaps then asked Dostler if the order came from a higher echelon (possibly Field Marshal Kesselring?), but because of the technical difficulties, Dostler's response was conveniently garbled.

Minutes after Klaps concluded his call with Dostler, his phone rang. It was *Oberst* Almers, ordering Klaps *not* to call headquarters again—and he was to drop the matter *immediately*. Dostler didn't appreciate being pressed by a *Kriegsmarine* intelligence officer questioning him at four thirty in the morning. Almers added that officers "which do not comply with those orders come before a court-martial." A few days later, Klaps sent a detailed report of Sessler's interrogations to *Oberst* (Colonel) Otto Helfferich, *leiter* (chief) of Military Intelligence Station Italy.

A notation here about General Dostler:

At no time between his capture and his trial did Dostler deny passing along the order to execute the Ginny OGs. Those were his words throughout his trial. In his mind, and based on his interpretation of the Commando Order, "passing along" was massively different than *initiating* the order himself and could have a major influence on his sentence. He steadfastly maintained that, first, he was bound by the Hitler Oath that all soldiers in the German Army took in 1933 with the advent of Hitler and National Socialism, and that in turn had obliged him to obey the *Führer befehl* of October 18, 1942.

Anton Dostler was born in Munich, Germany, on May 10, 1891. In 1910 he joined the German Army as a junior officer. Between the start of WWII and 1940, Dostler served as chief of staff of the Seventh Army. Later he commanded the 57th Infantry Division and the 163rd Infantry Division. Then, after some temporary stand-ins at Corps, he was appointed commander of the 75th Army Corps with the position of *General der Infanterie* (general of the infantry), or lieutenant general.

Between 1934 and 1935, officers and men of the German Armed Forces and civil servants took an oath of allegiance pledging personal loyalty to Adolf Hitler. This oath replaced the oath of allegiance in Germany's constitution. Historians view the personal oath of the Third Reich as a watershed moment—an important psychological element that would enable soldiers to obey orders for committing war crimes, atrocities, and genocide.

During the Nuremberg Trials, many German officers unsuccessfully attempted to use that oath as a defense against charges of war crimes and crimes against humanity. Dostler claimed that since he was abiding by the Hitler Oath of 1933, he had no choice but to obey Hitler's Commando Order. Like it or not, Dostler said, he was obeying the orders he had sworn to follow. He took this defense to his trial after the war. Of course it did not work.

Besides the efforts of Klaps and Sessler, another officer at headquarters, 75th Army Corps, had made a dangerous and ultimately unsuccessful attempt to save the lives of the Ginny OGs. He did not fare as well as the other officers.

Rittmeister d.r. (Reserve Cavalry Captain) Alexander Fürst zu Dohna-Schlobitten, GSO 3 (intelligence officer), was appointed to Dostler's staff at 75th Army Corps. His name translated to "Alexander, Prince to zu Dohna of Schlobitten," the name of his ancestral home. An impressive name; he also had extraordinary Nazi connections—despite his refusal to join the Nazi Party. He was a friend of *SS-Obergruppenführer* Karl Wolff, Supreme SS and Police Leader (*Höchster SS-und Polizeiführer, HöSSPF*) and an SS functionary in Italy who served as Chief of Personal Staff to *Reichsführer-SS* Heinrich Himmler. Wolff at one time was also an SS liaison between Himmler and Adolf Hitler. Wolff ended the war as the Supreme SS and Police Leader in occupied Italy. He helped arrange for the early surrender of Axis forces in that theater, effectively ending the war there several days sooner than in the rest of Europe. At the Nuremberg Trials, Wolff escaped prosecution, apparently because he had participated in Operation Sunrise, a series of secret negotiations in March 1945 in Switzerland between Karl Wolff and the US Office of Strategic Services (OSS) under Allen Dulles. In 1962 Wolff was prosecuted in West Germany for the deportation of Italian Jews and was sentenced in 1964 to fifteen years in prison as an accessory to murder. He was released in 1971 due to his failing health and died thirteen years later.

Wolff and zu Dohna had been classmates in high school. Through Wolff, zu Dohna gained a friendship with Himmler, one of the most powerful and notorious people under Hitler. This relationship, as we will see, would save zu Dohna's life—barely.

On February 1, 1944, as a cavalry captain, zu Dohna arrived at 75th Army Corps headquarters to act as Dostler's GSO 3 (intelligence officer), not as a staff officer.

Dostler was at first pleased with zu Dohna's appointment because he knew his former classmate had "friends in higher places," and he was a friend of the notoriously creepy Himmler, which Dostler figured might someday be helpful to him and his career. So he initially handled zu Dohna with kid gloves.

Zu Dohna was serving as Dostler's intelligence officer in March 1944, the time the Ginny OGs came ashore, and had written in the LXXV's war diary that "the American commando troop captured the previous day were soldiers in uniform and should be treated as POWs, but that General Dostler thought they were saboteurs and had ordered them to be shot immediately."

It is apparent that not only did the OGs suffer the travails of their capture—which, yes, was their own fault—but they also had the bad luck of running afoul of a "wannabe Nazi general" and an equally Hitler-loyal General Dostler. This was tantamount to the defense in a civilian trial drawing the worst possible judge for their case. Such is the roll of the dice.

In 1989 zu Dohna published his autobiography. Zu Dohna's recollections of what happened at headquarters, 75th Army Corps, at San Andrea relating to the OGs on March 25 are vivid and detailed—a particularly meaningful high-altitude rendering of what occurred as seen by an involved eyewitness.

In the war diary, Alexander Fürst zu Dohna-Schlobitten wrote the following:

> On 23 [*sic*] March 1944 fifteen American soldiers landed in Bonassola on the Italian coast near La Spezia. In the Ginny OG group, they were an engineer officer, the leader of the troop, a pioneer officer, three NCOs, and ten enlisted men. They had been put ashore at night from a US fast boat [*Schnellboot*] which had departed from an American base in Corsica with the order to demolish a tunnel on the Genoa-Rome railroad. However, their mission failed. Since the Americans were regular soldiers and revealed themselves as such to Italian civilians, the latter brought them to a [German] commando, which consisted of an NCP and two men; never did [an enemy] commando, which consisted of an NCO and two men, allow itself to be captured more peacefully.
>
> Their interrogation was conducted by different units. I notified Colonel Albers [*sic:* Almers], the commander of the unit which held them, that the Americans should be taken to a POW camp in the rear area. At the same time, I reported the event to General Dostler as well as to General von Vietinghoff, the commander in chief of the Army to which the LXXV Corps was subordinate. General Dostler declared *that the prisoners were*

saboteurs and must be shot immediately and without trial pursuant to a secret order (Geheimfehl) [emphasis added]. I was so enraged over this order, which Chief of Staff Colonel [Kraehe] assigned me to transmit, that I refused to comply. This produced a heated discussion with Colonel Kraehe, for General Dostler was away again, having driven to the coast because of a toothache. I pointed out to him that the Americans were regular soldiers in full uniform, and two officers wore their appropriate rank insignia. Colonel [Almers] accepted my view. The Germans also mounted commando operation (*Soßstruppenternehmen*) by such an infringement of the Geneva retaliation against German soldiers.

Colonel [Kraehe] did not want to make the decision without Dostler, so the prisoners at first remained with the troops [emphasis added]. In the meantime, I sought in many telephone conversations to make sure of the support [of my view] from the division [*sic*] commander in whose area the Americans had given themselves up—unfortunately without success. After two days Dostler returned to the Corps headquarters and ordered the execution. My deputy, Second Lieutenant Werkshage, reported to the Army [?] that it [the execution] had been carried out. It was announced, in fully distorted fashion (*volkommen eutstellt)* literally, completely created in the following words: "The American sabotage troop, consisting of two officers and thirteen men, which landed on 23 March near Bonassola, was wiped out to the last man." Up until the last, I had hoped General Vietinghoff would intervene, but nothing happened.

Shortly afterward Colonel [Kraehe] told me that I would be dismissed from the Corps staff because of my refusal to obey an order. General Dostler had requested that I be immediately transferred and had entered a note in my personal file that I was politically unreliable (politisch unzuverlässig) [emphasis added]. I was sent home, where the political government assigned me to dig antitank ditches [in East Prussia]. In May 1944 I was dismissed from the Armed Forces with a notice that my name be stricken from the list of intelligence officers; I should not count on being recalled to active duty. If this event had happened after July 20, 1944 [the failed *Attentat* (attempted assassination of Hitler), after which many German officers were executed], it could have cost me my life. Here, also, a few officers in OKH protected me.

Zu Dohna's remark, "a few officers in OKH protected me," is notable and probably a shrouded reference to his friendships with *Reichsführer-SS* Heinrich Himmler and his old school mate *SS-Obergruppenführer* and Supreme SS and Police Leader (*Höchster SS-und Polizeiführer, HöSSPF*) Karl Wolff. He did not want to be associated with two nefarious individuals after the war, but in the interim, they were good to have in his pocket.

Having been headquartered in Rome, Wolff had his ear out for everything in Italy. Through his friendship, zu Dohna could not have had two more powerful men in Germany in his pocket—and Dostler certainly was mindful of this powerful relationship. The purpose of the Higher SS and Police Leader was to be a direct command authority for every SS and police unit in each geographical region, answering only to *Reichsführer-SS* Heinrich Himmler and Adolf Hitler. Wolff acted as the highest liaison under Himmler, a "unifier" for the SS and police command in Italy. It is assumed that Dostler knew this, and that only the idea of the Wolff-Himmler friendship would have caused Dostler to back off. He did not wish to stick his general's epaulets in a hornet's nest—wisely, it should be stated. Undoubtedly, without the Wolff-Himmler friendship, zu Dohna would have been found guilty of treason and possibly faced a firing squad. Dostler also knew how to pick his battles, and he was not about to pick a fight with a man who had such influential friends. It served zu Dohna well to have friends in high places.

Zu Dohna continued in his diary regarding the matter:

Thirty-two years later a film company, the Chronos-Films, Inc., Berlin, wanted to know if I had been the zu Dohna who, as Ic with LXXV Corps in Italy, had refused to order the executions of the American soldiers who had been captured near La Spezia in March 1944. I admitted this, and they offered to bring me to Berlin; they were planning to make a documentary film about

General Dostler. The Americans had filmed Dostler's trial and also his execution. After 30 years this film had become available, and Chronos had acquired the rights to it. At first it could not be shown because Dostler's widow was still alive and raised objections. But Chronos gave me the opportunity to watch the film: Dostler accepted his sentence with dignity and without any sign of fear of his imminent death. [See photo insert.]

During my reading of the old, long-forgotten documents, my perception of those events changed. In 1944 only the [1939] OKH (*Oberkommando des Heeres*) directive for the treatment of saboteurs was known to me; now, for the first time, I read the [Commando] order of October 18 1942 signed by Hitler himself, which had been top-secret (*Chefsache*) and not available to me [in March 1944]. It now became clear to me that the situation for General Dostler, to whom the order had been sent, had been other than as I had perceived it in 1944. The unsoldierly and inhumane decree classified Allied soldiers on commando operations as saboteurs; it made no difference whether or not they were in uniform. Without qualification they were to be liquidated [*Laut Befehl mußten sie liquidiert warden*]. Sending the prisoners to a POW cage, as I had wanted, would have been senseless [*sinnlos*], because they would have been handed over to the SD [*sic*] and thus, in any case, shot. *If General Dostler had not carried out the Führerbefehl, it would have meant a court-martial and sentence for him* [emphasis added]. That would not have helped the American prisoners.

That General Dostler passed on to me to transmit so very serious a decision as the order to execute the fifteen Americans shows only how little human life—at least that of the enemy—meant to him. That he should have assumed responsibility never occurred to him. I believe that General Dostler and Colonel Kraehe acted without much thought. At that time they allowed the terrible automatic obedience (*der schrecklich Kadavergborsam*) to take over. This made such decisions easy.

In his pretrial testimony, Dostler persisted in giving the impression that he was not at San Andrea, his headquarters, on March 25—the day the fate of the Ginny OGs was hanging in the balance. As we have seen in zu Dohna's memoirs, Dostler was in Genoa with his mistress for most of the day. Therefore, the chronology of events as they unfolded in Dostler's testimony is filled with uncertainty and disconnection and will probably never be straightened out.

This uncertainty and disconnection are evident throughout the OG matter. According to the German perception of "strict obedience," some officers had second thoughts about the executions and the unswerving matter of obedience to Führer and Fatherland. This included Klaps, Sessler, and Körbitz, who seem to have been concerned with the morality of the matter—despite the austere *Führerbefehl*. Dostler, however, a fervent "Nazi general," was having second thoughts only because of his career. Whether he allowed the order or had it rescinded, his concern was not mainly the lives of fifteen men but of himself and his future as a German general and how he was perceived in the Nazi hierarchy. He was undoubtedly trying to make sure "his ass was covered" and had to be wholly convinced that his order—to execute or not to execute—would be approved all the way up the chain of command, including Adolf Hitler, who would undoubtedly hear about the matter.

At this point, with Klaps, Sessler, and Körbitz trying at the very least to postpone the execution, Colonel Kraehe, filling in for the absent Dostler, ordered zu Dohna, as the intelligence/counterintelligence officer, to order *Oberst* Almers to proceed with the executions.

Zu Dohna refused this order—an audacious, noble move—and we have seen what happened to him. After his return from Genoa, the order to execute came from either Kraehe or Dostler—more likely Dostler.

At Dostler's trial, the closing remarks of his attorney (Colonel Wolfe) appeared to show that Kesselring had almost certainly confirmed Dostler's order to proceed with the executions, which Dostler obediently did. However, Wolfe erred when he cited a paragraph from *The Rules of Land Warfare*, edition October 1940, reading for the Commission that "enemy soldiers were not to be punished for war crimes when a superior officer or his government had sanctioned the action." He was unaware that this passage had been revised in November 1944 to counter the "obedience-to-superior-orders" defense that many saw coming in the Nuremberg war crimes trials. Yet he found significance in a soldier's duty to obey when he told the Commission: "This time we won the war; next time we might not win it. Next time you gentlemen might be sitting [in the defendant's chair] and the victorious enemy might be sitting [where you are now]."

Wolfe hoped that the evidence he presented would result in only imprisonment for Dostler—not execution. It was not to be.

At 1600 hours, October 11, the jury retired to deliberate Dostler's fate. The next day, at 0900 hours, the president announced that they had found Anton Dostler guilty of the charge and specification.

The Commission did not find any mitigating circumstances in the matter. They sentenced Dostler to be "shot to death by musketry," an odd, antique word from the French *mousquetaire*, dating back to 1640–1650 and meaning "the technique of bringing fire from a group of rifles and automatic weapons to bear on specified targets."

Many US Army officers in the gallery gasped when they heard the sentence. To many, it meant that a general officer could lose his life for obeying an order when the result was determined to be a war crime. Some were not happy with the result. A sense of injustice had crept through the proceedings.

On October 24 Dostler filed a petition listing several reasons he believed the evidence should be reexamined and claiming that the *Füh rerbefehl* should be put into evidence along with the Supplement to Hitler's *Kommandobefehl*. He claimed that it had been extremely pivotal in determining his decision, which could be proven through interrogations of other German generals in POW stockades. The other egregious matter, he protested, was the absence at the trial of key witnesses who had not been located and so could not testify on his behalf.

Hitler's words in the Supplement served to enhance, or drive home, Dostler's duty to obey the command and execute the OGs.

Here is Hitler's Supplement to the Commando Order:

SUPPLEMENT TO COMMANDO ORDER OF 18 OCTOBER 1942

Notice on distribution—This order is not to be distributed behind the battalion and equivalent staffs of the other branches of the armed forces. After having been noted, copies distributed beyond the regiments and the equivalent staff of the other branches of the armed forces are to be collected and destroyed.

[initial] W [Warlimont]

[Handwritten] On February 25 43) M 9160 copy sent to Air Force High Command (Air Force Legal Dept., 5/12/43 copy to Qu (Admin. 2). On 5/4/44 1 Copy to Armed Forces Legal Dept. on 2/6.

[Handwritten] Note—Upon [telephone request from adjutant to the Reich Leader (Miss Fenske, Berghof 370)] and after conference with Chief Qu. Distribution of eight copies to subordinated office approved according to request, and with instructions that these offices must collect and destroy all copies which have been distributed further down, if any.

17/11 [Initials] Ki [Kipp]

[Translation of Document 503-PS]

Prosecution Exhibit 125

Letter from OKW, October 19, 1942, remaining Supplement to Commando Order signed by Hitler

[stamp] Top-Secret

High Command of the Armed Force

ARMED Force Operation Staff/Quartermeister [*sic*]

No. 55 1781/42 Top-Secret
Matter for Chiefs
Füehrer Headquarters, October 19 1942
22 Copies—21st copy
[Stamp] Top-Secret
Through officer only
As an addition to the decree concerning the destruction of terror and sabotage units (OKW/Armed Forces Operational Staff No. 003830/42 Top-Secret, dated October 18 1942) a supplementary order of the Führer is enclosed.

The order is intended for commanders only and must not under any circumstance fall into enemy hands.

The further distribution is to be limited accordingly by the receiving agencies.

The agencies named in the distribution list are held responsible for the return and distribution of all distributed copies of the order and extra copies made thereof.

By order:
The Chief of the High Command of the Armed Forces
[signed] Jodl

1 enclosure

Distribution:
General Staff of the Army, 1st copy
Chief of Army Armament and Command or Replacement Army, 2nd copy
High Command of the Navy, Naval War Staff, 3rd copy
High Command of the Air Force Operations Staff, 4th copy
Armed Force Commander Norway, 5th copy
Armed Force Command of Netherlands, 6th copy
Armed Force Commander Southeast, 7th copy
Armed Force Commander Ukraine, 9th copy
Commander in Chief West, 10th copy
20th Mountain Army, 11th copy
Commander of German Troops in Denmark, 12th copy
Commander in Chief South, 13th copy
Panzer Army Africa, 14th copy
German General with the Italian High Command, 15th copy
Reich Leader SS and Chief of German Police and Main Office of the Security Police, 16th and 17th copies
Office Foreign Counterintelligence, 18th copy
Air Forces Legal Department, 19th copy
Air Forces Propaganda, 20th copy
Armed Force Operations Staff, Quartermeister [*sic*] (draft, in 21st copy)
War Diary, 22nd copy

[stamp]

Top-Secret

Through officer only

The Füehrer and Supreme Commander of the Armed Force
October 18, 1942

I have been compelled to issue a strict order for the destruction of enemy troops and to declare noncompliance with this order severely punishable. I deem it necessary to announce to the competent commanding officers and commander the reasons for this decree.

In this war as in no previous one, a method has been developed of destruction of communications behind the front, intimidation of the populace working for Germany, as well as the destruction of war-important industrial plants in territories which we have occupied.

In the East, as early as last winter, this type of combat in the form of partisan warfare led to severe encroachments upon our fighting strength and cost the lives of numerous German soldiers, railroad workers, member of the Organization Todt, the labor service, etc. It severely interfered with, and sometimes delayed for days, the transportation necessary for the maintenance of the fighting strength of the troops. By a successful continuation, or perhaps even intensification, of this form of warfare, a grave crisis might develop at one or another point along the front. Many measures against these cruel as well as insidious sabotage activities have failed, simply because the German officer and his soldiers were unaware of the great danger confronting them and, therefore, in individual cases did not act against these enemy groups as would have been necessary in order to help the forward echelons at the front and thereby the entire conduct of the war.

It was, therefore, to some extent necessary to organize special units in the East who mastered this danger, or to assign this task to special SS formations.

Only where the fight against this partisan nuisance was begun and executed with ruthless brutality were results achieved which eased the situation on the fighting front.

In all Eastern Territories, the war against the Partisans is, therefore, a struggle for absolute annihilation of one or the other side.

As soon as the realization of this fact becomes common knowledge among the troops, they will regularly be able to cope with these occurrences quickly; otherwise, their effort will achieve no decisive results and will become purposeless.

England and America have decided upon a similar kind of warfare even though under a different name, while the Russians attempt to put partisan troops behind our font via the land routes and only in exceptional cases use air transportation to land men and supplies. England and America use this method of warfare primarily by landing sabotage troops from submarines or pneumatic rubber boats, or by dropping parachute agents. Essentially, however, this form of warfare does not differ from the activities of the Russian Partisans. For it is the task of these units—

1. To build up a general espionage service with the assistance of willing indigenous inhabitants.
2. To organize groups of terrorists and supply them with the necessary weapons and explosives.
3. To undertake sabotage activities which, by the destruction of traffic installation not only continuously disrupt our communication but also, when things become serious, make troop movement absolutely impossible and eliminate our communications system.

Finally, these units are to make attacks on war-important installations, in which, according to scientifically worked out programs, they blow up key plants, thereby forcing whole industries into idleness.

The consequences of these activities are extraordinarily serious. I do not know whether every commander and office is aware of the fact that the destruction of one single electric power plant, for instance, can deprive the air force of many thousands of tons of aluminum, thereby eliminating the construction of countless aircraft; these aircraft will be lacking at the front, and in this way serious damage will result to the homeland as well as bloody casualties to the fighting soldier.

Yet this form of war is completely without danger for the adversary. Since he lands his sabotage troops in uniform and at the same time supplies them with civilian clothes, they can appear as soldiers of civilians according to need. While they themselves have orders ruthlessly to eliminate German soldiers or even indigenous inhabitants who get in their way, they run no danger of suffering really serious losses in their operations, since at the worst, if they are caught they can immediately surrender and thus, as the thing theoretically falls under the provisions of the Geneva Convention. There is no doubt, however, that [this] is misuse in the worst form of the Geneva agreements, especially since most of these elements are even criminals liberated from prisons, who can rehabilitate themselves through these activities.

England and America will always be able to find volunteers for this kind of warfare, as long as these volunteers can be rightly told that their life is not imperiled. At worst, all they have to do is to attack people, traffic installations, or other installations successfully, and upon being encountered by the enemy to surrender.

If the German conduct of war is not to suffer grievous damage through these incidents, it must be made clear to the adversary that all sabotage units will be exterminated without exception to the last man [emphasis added].

This means that the chance of escaping with their lives is nil. Under no circumstance can it be permitted, therefore, that dynamite, sabotage, or a terrorist unit simply allows itself to be captured, expecting to be treated according to the rules of the Geneva Convention. This unit must under all circumstances be ruthlessly exterminated [emphasis added].

This report on this subject appearing in the armed forces communiqué will briefly and laconically state that a sabotage, terror, or destruction unit has been exterminated to the last man.

I, therefore, expect the commanding officers of armies as well as individual commanding officers not only to realize the necessity of taking such measure but also to carry out this order with all energy. Officers and noncommissioned officers who fail through some weakness are to be reported without exception, or in certain circumstances—when there is danger in delay—to be called to strict account at once. The homeland as well as the fighting soldiers at the front have the right to expect that behind their backs the essentials of nourishment as well as the supply of war-important weapons and ammunition remain secure.

These are the reasons for the decree I have issued.

If it should become necessary, for reasons of interrogation, to spare one or two men temporarily, then they are to be shot immediately after interrogation.

[Signed] Adolf Hitler

Dostler stated that crucial elements were missing from his defense: key witnesses, including Kesselring and Kraehe, whom he had requested but who had not appeared, and the Supplement in which it was stated that it was his duty to obey Hitler's orders. He therefore felt that it was not *his* order that had caused this "unfortunate incident," but the order that had come from "the head of state," Adolf Hitler.

Because of these elements, he requested that his sentence be reduced to imprisonment, or that his execution be suspended until the missing witnesses could be found and give their evidence.

All of this was denied.

CHAPTER 6

Those Big Trucks

ON APRIL 1, 1944, BRIGADE ALMERS'S 2,593 MEN, 41 OFFICERS, AND 394 NCOs were responsible for the defense of 70 craggy kilometers of the colorful Ligurian coastline. For centuries, Romans young, old, and infirm had trudged here and recreated in the warm sun, relishing the saline-scented air and munching on olives and salty sardines.

Since October 1943, 1st Company, Fortress Battalion 905, had been stalwart along the right bank of the River Magra, which separates the alluring peninsula and Liguria from historic Tuscany.

Here, the Ginny OGs will be executed with alacrity by some. Others were not so enthused about shooting uniformed soldiers as they might a bothersome elk in a dank forest back home. German boys with long rifles would follow orders and shoot American boys dead. Following orders is what this is about.

Hauptmann (Captain) Rudolph Bolze, 1st Company's *Kompaniechef* (commanding officer), was at his company's headquarters desk in Villa Angelo, just north of Bocca di Magra. He had had his breakfast, lunch, and dinner and now tended to humdrum paperwork. Bolze was a seasoned German officer. He was twenty-nine in 1944, had served with the 24th Regiment, 21st Infantry Division on the Russian front, and had joined the 905 Fortress Battalion in Sardinia in July 1943. After a move to Pisa in September, he went to Punta Bianca in October and was captured with his company at the Giovi Pass, north of Genora, in April 1945.

Today, March 25, a deadly day, Bolze's phone jingles at 1700 hours. He answers and receives an order from brigade headquarters (this would be *Oberst* Almers' brigade calling the *Hauptmann* with important instructions on a day never to be forgotten.

The caller orders Bolze to select a site in his company area on the Punta Bianca peninsula, where, centuries ago, the Romans had lolled in the sun. The site, the caller says, is going to be necessary for the burial of "some dead" saboteurs. The caller states with specificity that the burial site must measure "three meters wide by one and a half deep and six meters long."

Okay, thinks Bolze; we can do that. Although this is an extraordinary request, Bolze gets to it.

Ordering the taking of a bridge or a town or outflanking a squad of American soldiers; he has heard those orders before. But Bolze has never received a request to dig a grave of any type. In his mind he sees something more like a ditch, long and narrow, than a grave—almost like a foundation for a small edifice. He accurately assumes this grave is for many dead people—American soldiers?

He buttons up his tunic and brushes off a few dinner crumbs. He knows just the place. He has his *Oberleutnant* start up their staff car, an Opel four-seater with a Horch V-8 and an 80 hp engine, and they drive to the spot Bolze has in mind.

The site rests in opposition to a German ammunition dump near Ferrara—a place far from the populace, just in case, God forbid, it should accidentally ignite and blow up half the coastline. This is a place that stores lethal 88mm artillery shells that rip people, towns, and airplanes to unrecognizable pieces. But it is a good, lonely spot. Perfect for digging a massive grave today.

Bolze hastily assigns a *Feldwebel* (sergeant) to organize a work party of Italian laborers to start cutting and scrabbling the Italian soil where the Italian American OGs will rest forever. Soon enough, Italians are humping away at the gravesite, which takes no time to achieve the prescribed dimensions.

Last night, Bolze took more calls from Brigade. He deduced that the "saboteurs" were "many Americans." The working party he had been ordered to assemble must stand by and be available at 0600 hours the next morning. At the given time, he obediently waits with a *Feldwebel* and six men, standing idle approximately 250 meters from the open pit—the portentous gravesite.

For thirty minutes they are tense—smoking, spitting bits of tobacco off their tongues, throwing rocks at tree trunks. The digging has not taken them long, but they know now how serious this is, what will soon transpire. No simple task for any man, soldier or not. Just because they are Americans and foes of the Fatherland and wear different uniforms, executing innocents while looking into their eyes will not be easy. It could make a man cry. Do they know what's going on here? Truly little, particularly the NCOs. But the officers understand the enormity of the matter and the cat's cradle of obeying orders. They know that *Befehl ist Befehl.* ("An order is an order" is the standard German defense at Nuremberg.)

They are starting to see possible collusion.

Is this legal?

Two German officers in a camouflaged Auto-Union/Horch staff car (more prestigious than Bolze's, it can hold eight people) pull up to *Hauptmann* Bolze and interrupt his deliberations. In the car's passenger seat is *Hauptmann* (Captain) Wilhelm Rehfeld, *Bataillonskommandant* (Commander) 906th Fortress Battalion, commanding officer of the execution detail; accompanying him is an *Oberleutnant* (first lieutenant) at the steering wheel.

Trailing behind the Auto-Union/Horch are two Mercedes-Benz two-ton trucks—bruisers, swaying and bouncing on the dirt road—burdened with the precious load they bear. The sides are covered with tarps for secrecy.

Bolze dutifully tells Rehfeld that the grave that had been ordered is ready. Rehfeld replies that the Americans in the truck are alive and should be shot as soon as possible. But first, Bolze will have to take him to a suitable place for the executions. Just like that, like ordering a round of beers and bratwurst for the boys at the local bar.

Okay. It shall be.

Bolze squeezes into the back seat of the staff car, and they drive off toward Punta Bianca, leaving a swirl of questions in their wake. They leave the burial crew behind and drive two kilometers to Ferrara. The trucks, ponderous buffaloes, lag behind the staff car.

The Auto-Union/Horch stops, and Rehfeld suddenly, as if remembering he left his keys at the office, states that the executions cannot take place without the presence of a medical doctor—part of the prescribed procedures—a detail he should have arranged before driving out here. German efficiency, for the moment, has dropped off the table.

The OGs' deaths must be postponed while someone fetches a German military medical *doktor*.

Rehfeld sends the *Oberleutnant* off to battalion headquarters at Pugliola. It is five kilometers away near La Spezia, a ten-kilometer round-trip in the open-topped staff car that will take thirty minutes.

While they wait for the doctor's arrival, Bolze asks Rehfeld why he (Bolze) was chosen for this task. Rehfeld shrugs his shoulders; he has no idea. "Maybe you just picked up the phone at the wrong time."

Now they scout two locations for the executions, Bolze not only mulling over sites for suitability for the killings but also pondering a much more severe scenario for himself: his participation in a potential war crime. Bolze correctly assumes that what is going on here is evolving into a criminal undertaking—but one he must accept without objection, he being an officer in the Wehrmacht who has sworn allegiance to Führer and Fatherland. A pledged duty to obey "superior" orders. He is starting to think he should not have answered the phone. Neither Bolze nor Rehfeld has read or heard about Hitler's Commando Order. Pertinent now is *Befehl ist Befehl*—an order is an order. And so it shall be.

It was *Oberst* Almers who had received and passed along Dostler's order to execute the OGs. It was *Hauptmann* Rehfeld, at the lowest level of the chain of command, who was "following orders"—in turn, assigning Bolze to "follow orders" and organize the killing of these prisoners from America, who will be shot by riflemen who are also "following orders." It is starting to become a nettlesome issue for Bolze—how can anyone not think of it that way—and he is smart enough to know that what is occurring here could make him a war criminal. He could be prosecuted for his involvement. What could be correct about killing soldiers without a trial who have caused no harm here? He could be looking at a hangman's noose swaying in the air.

Rehfeld chooses one of the locations. This one. Under my shiny officer's boot, *Herr Hauptmann*.

He tells Bolze that he plans to line up the OGs facing the sea, their backs against a rocky cliff, adding that he will have the riflemen, the executioners, shoot the prisoners in two batches.

Bolze disagrees, saying bullets might ricochet off the rocks and injure the firing squad. Instead, he respectfully suggests, the OGs' backs should be *facing* the sea—in other words, facing the riflemen. Rehfeld agrees.

The trucks come to a lumbering halt near the site Rehfeld has selected; all are now assembled neatly about one hundred yards from the execution area, the place where blood will soon sully the soil. In a sworn statement after the German surrender, Bolze said he looked inside one of the trucks and saw prisoners in "brown uniforms with their hands tied behind their backs on two of them."

About twenty helmeted Germans guard them, scattered among the Mercedes trucks and the prisoners. In his statement, Bolze added that he was "not required to be present when they were shot." Instead, finding the matter abhorrent, he lights a cigarette and walks twenty meters away. He does not see the prisoners leave the trucks.

At 0715 hours, Dr. Heinz Kellner, a German officer and medical doctor (*Stabsarzt*) arrives at the site in his shiny black Opel. Kellner and Bolze speak for half a minute, exchange perfunctory salutes, and the doctor drives off to the execution site.

The fifteen Ginny OGs are still inside the trucks, their hands shackled behind them for what must be about an hour. Imagine that. They have to wait this whole time while the Germans get their ducks quacking in harmony, fetching a doctor who should have been here first thing.

A few days ago the OGs landed in Italy—a land of legend and culture, of Caesars and history, of flying bullets and exploding grenades. Now look at them—waiting, pondering their deaths and wearing the same uniforms they had on when they left Corsica. But because of their inept camouflaging of the dinghies—it needs to be said—here they are, sitting in silence with their tortuous thoughts. Also inexplicable: Why did Lieutenant Russo so carelessly approach Franco Lagaxo and his mother on March 24? This action broke a cardinal rule for soldiers operating in enemy territory: Never, never, reveal yourself to the natives unless they are known and have been verified as friendly. None of the OGs knew Lagaxo.

The German soldiers inside the trucks with the prisoners are in full combat gear and wearing dull black steel helmets. The Germans bear both the ubiquitous 7.62mm *Gewehr* (rifle) 41 and the infamous MP 40 "*Schmeisser*" machine pistols. It is not known which weapon the guards will use to shoot the OGs: The 7.62 Gewehr is a bolt-operated rifle, the *Schmeisser* an automatic machine pistol. Some of the guards in the trucks have not even graduated high school. Führer and Fatherland hooked them first.

All in the truck, German and American alike, are undoubtedly thinking the same damned thing: *How the fuck can we get away from this!*

God rarely favors miracles, and only a miracle will save them now. That's not going to happen.

At 0715 Bolze, still a short distance from the site, hears the sharp whack of riles firing in unison—a volley from the *Gewehr* 41s. Ten rifles firing simultaneously, he estimates. It sends a shiver down his spine.

At 0720 another explosive volley takes down the last of the fifteen—all the OGs have been executed.

An autopsy report after the war erroneously stated that the OGs' skulls were shattered. This led to the belief that they had been beaten to death with either shovels or rifle butts. However, a subsequent autopsy report determined that the shattered skulls were probably due to a coup de grâce, assuring their deaths.

Bolze said that he went to the execution site, which took about one minute's walking time to reach. He made no mention of coup de grâce shots. They probably occurred before he reached the dead prisoners.

And here is Dr. Kellner performing his medical duty, checking the bleeding, shattered bodies. Bolze could see that the OGs had their backs facing the sea as he had suggested. From fifteen meters away, he could see that not all were dead; blood was spurting from the wounds in some of the second group. All the bodies were still clothed in their US uniforms—leggings and field jackets on the OGs.

German soldiers from Bolze's company come over to investigate the gunfire. They're curious, like people stopping to view the aftermath of an auto crash. Bolze apologizes for not warning them that a "special event" was taking place. He does not believe they have seen what has occurred. Four or five more German soldiers approach; he tells them the same thing.

Bolze finishes talking with the curious group and walks back to the execution site. There, the firing squad uses wooden planks like stretchers to load the bodies aboard one of the trucks, which had been turned around to allow easy access for the bodies.

Bolze calls a few men over from the De Lutti battery and orders them to clean up the blood. He notices that some of the bodies do not have their boots on; they have been thrown into the truck. He does not understand why the boots have been removed from some of the Americans.

The bloody area is finally cleaned up, and Bolze, riding in Rehfeld's staff car, heads back to the burial site near Ferrara. There he watches the bodies be transferred from the trucks to the open grave.

After the war Bolze testified that "all military conventions were followed" except that the grave was not marked. Dr. Heinz Kellner, present when the OGs were shot, told Bolze that "the Americans died calmly and quietly and bravely."

The remains of the first group's bodies are aligned inside the trucks. The other group, a few feet away, wait for burial.

Chapter 7

The Bodies in the Ditch

On April 22, 1945, investigators from OSS Secret Intelligence Italy had been investigating the fate of the Ginny OGs. On that same date, they received information about the missing OGs through Giovanni Zolesi, a twenty-year-old Italian civilian at the Refugee Camp of La Marmora in Rome.

Zolesi was born four kilometers northeast of Punta Bianca and had worked for TODT, Germany's civil and military engineering organization named for *Generalmajor* (Major General) Fritz Todt, an engineer and senior Nazi. Although Zolesi did not witness the executions and could not provide specific details, he and several others were in the area a few hours before the OGs faced the firing squad.

Zolesi provided an informative, detailed drawing of where the burial took place, which he said was approximately three hundred meters from a German ammunition dump. Across from the dump was a common grave where, he said, the American soldiers had been buried.

Three days later, on April 25, just hours after the Germans had left, Italian civilians came forward to tell what they knew and had heard about the burials. One, Mario fu Gradito, gave the following testimony in Ameglia. On April 26, he wrote:

> In my capacity as a keeper of the Ferrara powder magazine, on the morning of March 26, 1944, at about 8 o'clock, I went to my work as usual. When I arrived at a point about 200m. distant from the magazine, I was stopped [by a German sentinel]. It was the first time that a sentinel had been put on that spot. (I later learned that all roads of the approach to the magazine had been blocked.) I could see a parked truck within the limits of

the magazine; also, six soldiers filling up a ditch. Lino ZOLESI and Nunzi ABATI and I waited for almost an hour before being allowed to enter. Upon questioning the night watchman who had been kept in the guard room all morning, I learned that a German truck loaded with an unknown number of bodies had arrived in the morning. The bodies had been buried in a ditch dug the night before by workers of the TODT organization. The workers had been told that the ditch would be used as an ammunition dump. When I visited the burial place, I observed that the ditch was easily found because the fresh earth covering it had been camouflaged with tree branches. I also noticed two large blood pools. A few days later, a German soldier told me, in the presence of Alessandro RAULF, at present in Milan, that the bodies were those of fifteen American soldiers who had been captured in the vicinity of La Spezia. After having been executed at the "De Lutti" battery at Punta Bianca, they were buried at the "Ferrara" powder magazine.

One day later, April 27, 1945, a team of investigators from SCI-Z followed Zolesi's directions and his detailed drawing. They found and photographed the site but did not attempt to disturb the grave. About a month later—why it took so long is unknown—an OSS team led by Captains Albert G. Lanier and Nevia Manzani arrived at the site to uncover the grave.

Captain Lanier had been one of the OSS officers assigned in April to find out what happened to the OGs. At a POW cage (prison) on May 1–3, 1945, he had interrogated former German *Oberleutnant* (1st Lieutenant) Rudolph Bolze, whom we have heard from extensively.

With Bolze's eyewitness account in hand, Captain Lanier sought the gravesite. He had had marked the general area of the grave on a Michelin road map—it was on the Punta Bianca peninsula, an isolated area. He arrived at the Ferrara ammunition dump on May 20, 1945.

With him were OSS Captain Manzini and two physicians: Maj. G. M. Bassett and Capt. R. J. Willoughby, who had been stationed at the 103rd Station Hospital in Pisa since April 23. Lanier was also accompanied by 1st Lt. R. L. Mosely, SSgt. E. L. Ferris, three enlisted men from US Graves Registration, and nine robust Italian laborers.

Staff members from Graves Registration and the local laborers helped excavate the grave on May 20, 1945. It took them three days to locate the bodies, which were at the bottom of an elongated trench, fifteen feet below the road's surface.

Each American had his hands tightly secured behind their backs with wire. Several were not wearing shoes or socks. Most still wore their olive drab military shirts, trousers, and jackets. Three of the bodies had no outer clothing. These notations were subsequently interpreted to mean that the Ginny OGs had been "robbed" of their clothing, which was untrue.

Remember the minor skirmish the Germans had with the OGs right after Materazzi was found to have a pistol? First, it is common in situations where prisoners show a strong desire to escape to remove their shoes and socks; this prevents or hinders them from running away. Some of their shirts and outer clothing had been removed to prevent them from hiding any weapons. For years this was misinterpreted as "signs of torture" committed by the Germans. And because the remains had shattered skulls with no bullet holes (the prisoners had been shot in the torso), the OSS mistakenly interpreted these as signs of torture as well.

Before removing the corpses, Captain Lanier drew a diagram showing the positions of the remains. He made meticulous notes of what he observed. Lanier, Major Bassett, and Captain Willoughby then repeated the inspection of the site and the remains, adding to the notes and burning the details into their minds.

At the time of exhumation, seven bodies were positively identified:

a) Body No. 1—By laundry markings. It was identified to be T/5 Angelo Sirico, 32533008.
b) Body No. 2—By laundry markings on drawers, it was identified to be T/5 Joseph A. Libardi, 31212732.
c) Body No. 5—By T/Sgt. Stripes on OD shirt and size of body, it was identified to be T/Sgt. Livio Vieceli, 33037797.
d) Body No. 7—By two large plates, it was identified to be Sgt. Alfred De Flumeri, 31252071.

e) Body No. 8—By laundry marking on drawers and by Sgt. stripes, it was identified to be Sgt Dominic C. Mauro.

f) Body No. 11—By dog tags and laundry marking on drawers, it was identified to be T/5 Joseph Noia, 32536119.

All were positively identified as the Ginny OGs and members of Unit A, 1st Contingent. According to Lanier, this was done by comparing dental and medical records. How that was possible is unknown, because Lanier did not have those records with him at the gravesite; they were locked up at Company A. It seems that Lanier was going to ID the bodies as the OGs no matter what.

The group also checked laundry marks, dog tags, NCO chevrons, and physical characteristics, which Lanier claimed were known to him. Again, how was this done? Lanier had never seen the OGs in person before. Also, there is no evidence to show that Lanier brought any medical records or comparative documentation with him to the gravesite. So how could Lanier, a lawyer, have been so positive about identifying fifteen men who had been interred and decomposing for nearly twelve months?

The remains were taken to Forte dei Marmi, situated between Punta Bianca and Viareggio. There, on May 27, 1945, they were examined a second time, by Major Pedro M. Souza, MC, the medical officer of the Italian OGs, 2671st Battalion.

This is an extract from Souza's report:

Upon examination I found that the fifteen bodies had extensive fractures (unilateral) of the temporal bone; the opposite temporal bones were intact. This excludes the possibility of the personnel having been shot in the head. The bodies showed no bullet perforation (thorax, abdomen, and extremities). Also, the clothing did not show any perforation that could have been caused by a bullet. In my opinion in all fifteen cases, death was caused by severe traumatism in the temporal region, extensive fracture of the temporal bone, severe brain injury, and hemorrhage.

Lanier must have been having eye issues that day. Captain Lanier, a lawyer, had somehow convinced himself that he had not seen any evidence that the Germans had not shot the OGs but had instead beaten them with shovels. Souza tacitly agreed, neither wanting to see what the destructive force to the skull can be.

Plentiful, too, were the prejudicial, even irresponsible, details Lanier used to described the victims in his notes. Here are a few examples:

T/5 Angelo Sirica "[right] side of face bashed in; jawbone broken. No sign of bullet holes;" T/5 Joseph A. Libardi, "[h]ead NOT [Lanier's emphasis] bashed in, three holes in back, possibly bullet holes"; T/5 Salvatore Di Scalfani: "[s]kull possible bullet holes."

Regarding Souza's autopsy report, it must be noted that the postmortem examinations he performed on the OGs' remains were considered substandard. Further, dental records of the deceased were on file at Company A, 267th Battalion, at Siena and were available to Dr. Souza. From his reports, it is apparent he did not use them.

Dr. Souza, and Lanier before him, managed to assign the wrong names to several corpses, which were buried with the wrong identities. A further exhumation and autopsy were made by a more competent pathologist. Today, every Ginny OG lies under his proper tombstone.

Both Souza and Lanier were now and forever responsible for both initiating and perpetuating a rumor that would enrage the OSS. The myth would be difficult to dispel and would dishonestly vibrate for many, many years: that the OGs had been beaten to death with shovels because their skulls were shattered and that their bodies had been robbed of several items of outer clothing and shoes. This is all fallacious.

A lawyer not a pathologist, Lanier apparently had no idea what shattering force a bullet can have on a skull at close range. One only has to go as far as President John F. Kennedy's autopsy to see the shattering, destructive force a bullet from a high-powered rifle can have—and that was fired from eighty-one yards, not close range. Sadly, the fallacy has been published as truth many times and might never abate.

Why?

Consider the worldwide events at that time: 1943–1945. The Germans were involved in unspeakable horrors, particularly the concentration camps, killing entire populations of small towns, and razing villages. The SS were committing horrendous war crimes throughout Europe. Against this backdrop, it seemed credible to Lanier and Souza—particularly Lanier—that the same "unspeakable" horrors, such as smashing heads with shovels, were not out of the question. Rather, it complied with the image the world had come to expect from the German military. Shooting soldiers was "humane" and certainly at the heart of warfare, not something the German "monsters" were capable of. Indeed, cracking heads with shovels and butts of rifles was more suitable and newsworthy behavior for them. Lanier thought that it would garner him more international press and uncover yet another German atrocity.

Captain Lanier forced himself to dismiss any emotion that might evolve during his viewing of the Ginny OGs' remains. Lanier knew he would earn a place in history through the telling of an atrocity that fell neatly, conceivably, among all the other atrocities of the time. After all, atrocities are much bigger news than executions via firing squads.

The "humane" act of shooting the OGs, and not the abhorrent act of beating them to death, was—conveniently or not—overlooked by the prosecution at Dostler's trial through the eyewitness testimony of *Obergefreiter* (Corporal) Wilhelm Knell, a member of Lieutenant Bolze's 1st Company, Fortress Battalion 905.

Knell was the only German in Allied custody who had been on Punta Bianca. He had witnessed the executions from nearby—his quarters had been on Punta Bianca. Since he knew he was not being charged with a crime, he had no vested interest in lying.

This is part of Knell's account of what he witnessed the day of the executions:

At 0600 hours [on March 26, 1944], I saw fifteen Americans under guard dismount from two trucks. This was at or near the 1st Company area [Punta Bianca] that I was only a few feet away from the prisoners. I did not recognize their uniforms because I was then unfamiliar with American army uniforms, but subsequent to that time I have learned to recognize American uniforms, and now I know that the prisoners were in such uniform. The American prisoners were taken to a point approximately 80 meters from the location of my billet. There is such that I could see the firing squad, but not the prisoners. I saw several German officers at the scene of execution but recognized only *Oberleutnant* Bolze. I believe Bolze turned and walked away from the scene before the first volley was fired. I saw the firing squad, which consisted of about 30 soldiers—one rank kneeling and one rank standing—fire the second volley immediately after the first volley was fired. I started down a path which led past the scene of execution on my way to obtain some coffee from a Navy unit stationed in the area. As I passed the scene of execution, *Oberleutnant* Bolze called me over to assist in the burial of seven or eight Americans who had been shot. I saw a tall German officer going from victim to victim, firing a shot from a pistol into the back of each skull [a coup de grâce]. Some [,] and possibly all [,] of the victims had their hands bound behind their back. . . . After assisting in the burial of the seven or eight Americans, I was directed by *Oberleutnant* Bolze to return to my company area. I did so return and there saw the firing squad fire a second volley, presumably at the remaining American prisoners.

Nowhere in Knell's narrative do we see Germans beating the Americans with shovels. And he was an eyewitness. Those infected with Germanophobia might want to disagree here, but facts are facts.

The evidence suggests that the Ginny OGs were executed by a "legitimate" military firing squad following German procedure and regulations for such an event and were not beaten to death as inferred by Lanier's misleading notes or Souza's incompetent autopsy.

⌁

Now, with most of the answers concerning the fate of the OGs falling into place, the OSS set out to show that war crimes had been committed and that apprehension and trial should be in order.

A good portion of helpful information came from none other than the OGs' primary interrogator, Georg Sessler of German Naval Intelligence.

On April 25, 1945, Sessler was in Milan when the Italian Partisans saw fit to launch a major insurrection against the Germans and the Fascist government. Known as a German intelligence officer, Sessler feared for his life and hastily crossed the Swiss border at Chiasso. On May 2 he contacted a Swiss friend who had contacts with British intelligence agents in Milan. He asked his friend to assist him in returning to Italy from Switzerland and to notify the British agents that he could be helpful. Georg Sessler was ready to cooperate with Allied intelligence officers, particularly regarding Dostler and the Ginny executions. On May 3 he returned to Milan and began a series of intelligence briefings with American and British officers. Two days later, he wrote down everything he knew about German intelligence in Italy. The report included the first mention of the OGs' executions. On May 12 the British sent Sessler to Florence, handing him over to Americans to interrogate for the first time on the Ginny OG case. In detail, Sessler recounted what he had witnessed at Punta Bianca. During this interrogation by the American officers, Sessler erroneously attributed the Americans' execution order to General Rudolf Toussaint, commissioner of the Wehrmacht in Italy at the time.

At the end of May, Sessler changed his story, explaining that he had erroneously named Toussaint as the general who ordered that the OGs be executed (why he did this is unknown). Rather, it was General Anton Dostler who had ordered the executions. At the time of Sessler's interrogation, Dostler was being held at a POW camp in Taranto, in southern Italy. The Americans took Dostler into their custody at the Combined Service Detailed Interrogation Center at the Cinecittà Studios movie complex. (Mussolini had inaugurated the complex in 1937. Large enough to house thousands of prisoners, it was the same studio where *Cleopatra*, starring Elizabeth Taylor, would be filmed in 1963.)

Much searching over the years has never produced a definitive document showing that Dostler issued the order himself to execute the Ginny OGs, ordered a subordinate to pass along his approval, or received tacit approval from Kesselring. It can, however, be safely assumed that this matter was certainly telexed from Kesselring to Hitler—and with further certainty that the document will never be found.

Why?

In pretrial testimonies and statements at Dostler's trial in Rome, several officers swore that an order had stated that all records associated with the Ginny OGs be destroyed—and that the time, the date, and so on, be included in the report to OBSW.

Here again, Georg Sessler fills in the picture with helpful details. In a pretrial statement, Sessler swore to the following:

> Two or three weeks [after the executions] an order was issued [from Colonel Helfferich, Chief of Military Intelligence Station Italy] according to which all material pertaining to this case has to be destroyed. [This order] demanded a statement of the completion of [the destruction]. This was confirmed by Klaps in his statement of June 13 1944. About 14, 15 days [after the executions], I received an order from the "Abwehrstelle Italy," in Borghetto [Colonel Helfferich's headquarters] according to which I had to destroy all the material pertaining to that case and to report the completion of same at a certain time. The Easter following Tuesday, or Wednesday, I learned from *"Oberleutnant von Tarbeck [Tarbuck]"* then acting for *"Oberst* Helfferich of the Abwehrstelle, Italy" that the destruction of the material to OB South-West. During an undated testimony Schultz swore: [Dostler's] instructions [to execute the Ginny OGs] were received thorough telegram and so far as I know [also] through telephone. I saw the telegram, I don' recall whether I saw the telegram that day [when it arrived] or a few days later when the papers were destroyed. I personally saw them destroyed.

It is apparent that, on one level, several of the younger officers felt sure that what they were engaged in was illegal but necessary because the illegality flowed down from Adolf Hitler to the *Führerbefehl* and to the men who had to follow the order to execute.

Before Dostler's trial, Westphal and Kesselring were in Nuremberg to testify as witnesses at the upcoming war crimes trials. Dostler wanted them in Rome to testify in his defense. This was denied. Why? No one seems to know or has provided a satisfactory answer. Perhaps the defense could have provided details in Dostler's favor and, possibly, saved his life. There is also the possibility that, if in Rome, either Westphal or Kesselring could have let slip a piece of evidence indicating Kesselring's order to execute the Ginny OGs. Being interrogated by a trial lawyer solely for this purpose would not have been the same as being questioned by Dostler's lawyers. Instead, Westphal and Kesselring were interrogated under oath in Nuremberg.

Major Robert E. Haythorne interrogated Westphal on October 4. This is an important portion of that interrogation:

Maj. Haythorne:	If the matter of the execution of these [Ginny Mission] soldiers had come to your headquarters, would you probably have known about it?
Westphal:	If it had come to my headquarters, I would have known about it.
Maj. Haythorne:	Do you recall or can you remember any incident, like the incident I have described, of the execution of the two officers and thirteen American soldiers?
Westphal:	I recollect now that such report had come along, that commando troops had been captured.
Maj. Haythorne:	What action was taken at your headquarters on that matter?
Westphal:	As far as I remember, an action to postpone this matter had been taken.
Maj. Haythorne:	Was it referred to OKW?
Westphal:	I think that the capture of the commando troops had been reported to the high headquarters, because all reports had gone straight to the OKW from all Army Groups, that is Army Groups South-West.

Maj. Haythorne:	Let me ask you again: Are you reasonably sure that it was this particular instance I have described?
Westphal:	I cannot say with certainty.
Maj. Haythorne:	Do you recall an order by OKW as to what was to be done with these troops?
Westphal:	It is very difficult for me to testify to this under oath, but I believe that an order had come down from OKW that these troops should be treated according to the Füehrer's decree. May I put it this way: That had it been reported that such troops had been captured, it could have been safely expected that the OKW would have sent in an order for these troops to be treated according to the Füehrer's decree.
Maj. Haythorne:	On what do you base your recollection that this matter was referred to OKW?
Westphal:	It has certainly been reported in the daily report of the Army Group von Zangen to us.
Maj. Haythorne:	Do you remember anything about it? Does it sound familiar to you now?
Westphal:	I think, yes. I already mentioned something about some troops in La Spezia, in Freising, without knowing anything more about it. I think that my testimony, that I have in Freising, must show this, because I said that we had tried to avoid the execution of these troops, at first in Ancona [a case involving the capture of British commandos], and then perhaps in La Spezia, too. I would say that I have a vague recollection of it. I must add that at that time I worked for 17 hours a day, and I, at that time, just went to the hospital, too. Later on, I still suffered from heavy blood poisoning, and I have to state that I know very little of what went on this half a year. Perhaps I may put it this way: I remember that commando troops landed near

La Spezia, and I think it is probable that such reports had been referred to the OKW.

Maj. Haythorne: Well, do you have a recollection in that instance of the reports having been forwarded?

Westphal: I cannot say exactly.

Maj. Haythorne: General, is there anything that you would like to say, whether I have asked you or not, to be used at General Dostler's trial, in his defense: If so, feel free to say it now.

Westphal: I want to say this: if the report, as I believe it was, had been given to the OKW, I am sure that the order to shoot these people came from OKW.

It should be noted that, in his testimony, Westphal had said, "May I put it this way: That had it been reported that such troops had been captured, it could have been safely expected that the OKW would have sent in an order for these troops to be treated according to the Füehrer's decree." This would have meant that the order to execute had come down through the chain of command and eventually landed on Dostler's desk.

On May 24 Colonel Livermore telexed Donovan in Washington, DC, summarizing the Ginny investigation's progress to date. His report stated that the Ginny men had been shot by order of *Oberst* (Colonel) Almers, who obeyed the imperative he received from his commanding officer, General Toussaint. The execution was ordered because the *Führerbefehl* stated that all officers were obliged to execute all persons engaging in sabotage.

Livermore quickly wrote back, asking: "Are the subordinate commanders and soldiers of the firing squad guilty of war crimes when they are carrying out orders of colonels and generals? The latter, if apprehended, will probably say they got orders from the higher-ups." In other words, where does it stop?

On the same day, Washington replied with the following:

Defense for superior orders NOT valid, although it may be construed for lenient sentences. All Implicated in crime, irrespective of rank, station, or involuntary character of their acts, are to be regarded as war criminals, and full information on all is required. For international trials, especially interested in all from Commissioned officers up as defendants. Soldiers of firing squads, etc., may be material witnesses in international trial and also defendants before American military commission. Army Field Manual 27-10 now being amended to conform to foregoing.

By the end of May, Sessler had revised his story. He explained that he had mistakenly named General Toussaint as the general who issued the execution order. Why? Actually, at this point no one knows precisely who ordered the execution of the Ginny OGs. Instead Sessler said that General Dostler, commanding general of the 75th Army Corps, had sent out the orders to execute.

Dostler was interrogated by Captain Blythin at Cinecittà Studios, the movie studio complex, on June 9, 1945. The interpreter, Alexander Goldodetz, was British American.

When asked, Dostler immediately recalled the incident. Word had come to him from Brigade Almers that fifteen captured Americans, Italian-speaking, were saboteurs. Dostler passed this information to his chief of staff and asked him to relate the details to General von Zangen, the group commander. Dostler wanted to know if this fell under Hitler's *Führerbefehl*, Hitler's order concerning the treatment of commando groups. The army group immediately replied with a curt "yes." Dostler said he then ordered that the men be executed.

Sessler did not recall whether von Zangen had passed the order himself or his chief of staff, Colonel Nagel, had given the order. Dostler said that he had read Hitler's *Führerbefehl*, and to him it appeared that this group of Americans came directly under that order. In the end, he said, they did, and since the Ginny OGs did fall into the definition of the *Führerbefehl*, they had been executed legally. Dostler had acted legally, according to German law, he claimed, not the new Anglo-Saxon law imposed by the Americans, and he should not be executed.

"I cannot remember the exact details," Dostler told Blythin. "All I do know is that I read the *Führerbefehl* at the time and that according to its wording, it seemed clear that these men were saboteurs as defined therein. I would not, however, assume the responsibility for having the prisoners shot but referred it to the Army, who took the decision."

During the interrogations, Dostler repeatedly emphasized these points. And he was eager to produce the *Führerbefehl*. He *wanted* the *Füh rerbefehl* admitted as evidence to show that he was, indeed, following the orders of a higher authority. Dostler believed that if the *Führerbefehl* was produced, it would show that he, a dutiful soldier, was simply obeying the orders of his Supreme Commander, Adolf Hitler.

On June 10 Colonel Livermore sent a telegram to Donovan: "I have interrogated General Dostler who commanded 75th Army Corps. He freely admits that he gave orders to *Oberst* Almers to have the Ginny men executed. He states that he was in compliance with the Hitler Order that all persons apprehended while engaging in sabotage would be executed. He also said he received the order from Army command von Zangen to execute them."

By June 3, Lieutenant Blythin had honed his list of suspects and gathered evidence and testimony from interrogations of German POWs.

Oberst Kurt Almers, former commanding officer, 135th Fortress Brigade, was already at Peninsula Base Station, in PWE (Prisoner of War Enclosure) 339. Almers had passed along Dostler's execution order to Rehfeld, who was at the lowest rung of the accountability ladder. Captured in Genoa, Almers was interned in Pisa; he escaped twice. Blythin learned where Almers had been hiding, but Almers was not there when the Allies arrived. He was never captured or seen again.

Oberleutnant (First Lieutenant) Rudolph Bolze, officer in the coast naval artillery unit, was in a cage (prison) in Ancona, Italy.

Klaps, former officer in coast artillery, or naval artillery, was now in custody at CSDIC, Rome.

The following Germans were still at large and wanted as either defendants or witnesses:

Rudolf Toussaint, Armed Forces Plenipotentiary in Italy, who allegedly gave or approved the order that resulted in the murder of the Ginny OGs.

General Gustaf von Zangen, CG, LXXXVII Corps through 1943–44, wanted for interrogation in connection with the murder of the OGs.

Captain Rehfeld, former commanding officer, 906th Fortress Battalion, wanted for murder, having been the officer in charge of the squad that shot the Ginny OGs at Punta Bianca.

Unterarzt (doctor) Heinz Kellner, former medical officer, 906th Fortress Battalion, wanted as a witness to the murder of the OGs.

At the top of Blythin's list was *Generalleutnant* (Lieutenant General) von Zangen, who had commanded Army Group von Zangen but at this time was not in custody: "Allegedly upon receipt of request from commanding general of the troops of the Ginny mission [,] von Zangen ordered that they be shot."

Next on the list was Lt. Gen. Anton Dostler, who gave orders that the OGs be shot. His order was temporarily withdrawn but later reinstated "after receiving instruction from high headquarters," ostensibly from von Zangen via his chief of staff, Kraehe.

Based on the interrogation and report of General Doster, "The opinion is ventured that the evidence at hand is more than enough to convict General [Dostler] of the unlawful killing of [the Ginny OGs]."

———

At this point in the narrative, it might benefit the reader if we paused and reviewed a summary of events beginning with the Ginny OGs' departure from Corsica on March 22, 1944, and then pass through their subsequent capture, execution, and exhumation at war's end.

This brief overview of the operation is put forth because of the complexities of the structure and chain of events that took place, primarily in the German chain of command, and the interpretation or misinterpretation of their officers' understanding of the draconian *Führerbefehl* issued by Hitler on October 18, 1942.

US Navy PT boats *210* and *214* from Motor Torpedo Boat Squadron 15 (aka Ron 15), docked at Bastia's Old Harbor, were delayed by forty-five minutes because of a faulty radar unit in one of the PT boats; after replacement, the boats departed at 1830 hours. With explosives and weapons, aboard were fifteen OSS OGs from Unit A/1st Company and three bright orange rubber boats they would use to paddle ashore once they arrived at the designated pinpoint on the Ligurian coast.

The PT boats were to arrive three hundred yards southwest of their pinpoint at 2300 hours to allow the OG shore party to transfer from the PT boats onto the rubber boats. They were to "be at the target prepared to commence their mission at 0030 on March 23." The basic plan from the previously failed Operation Ginny I was still sound: Land at the pinpoint in rubber boats and proceed to the target by following the natural ravine to the track, and neutralize the signal house. After an on-the-spot reconnaissance conducted by 1st Lt. Vincent Russo, the engineering officer and commander of the shore party, they would set either time-delay or contact fuses on the tracks. They would then return to the rubber boats, paddle back to the PT boats, and return to Bastia.

At 1830 hours the PT boats departed the Old Harbor at Bastia, going westward on the Ligurian Sea, and, four and a half hours later, reached the pinpoint, Stazione de Framura. Along the way they were further delayed several times in order to evade suspicious enemy radar sightings; neither enemy vessels nor aircraft were spotted visually.

Ginny I and, subsequently, Ginny II were failures in execution.

While the plan had been referred to as "risky," overall, it was feasible and had a good chance of success. However, the failure chain began in both missions with the PT boats arriving at the wrong pinpoint on the Ligurian coast and the OGs paddling to an incorrect disembarkation point. They became disoriented entirely because they were at the wrong spot and were floundering in the immediate area, trying to correct their errors. From here, the mission went haywire, and their errors began to compound and subsequently led to their capture and deaths. One of the most egregious mistakes was not effectively camouflaging the rubber boats, which were bright orange, making them quite visible in all forms of light.

Further, having captured the Ginny OGs, the Germans were having a particularly difficult time deciding which command—there were three— was responsible and who would take the fall if the right decision was not made regarding the execution of the OGs.

The captured OGs were brought to La Spezia and were confined in a stable near the 135th Fortress Brigade (Brigade Almers) headquarters, commanded by German *Oberst* (Colonel) Kurt Almers.

The next higher headquarters, to which Almers was subordinate, was *Generalkommando LXXV Armeekorps* (Headquarters LXXV Army Corps), whose commanding officer was *General der Infanterie* (General of the Infantry) Anton Dostler, a rank equivalent to a US Army lieutenant general.

The next higher headquarters was that of Army Group von Zangen, commanded by General of the Infantry von Zangen, who was called as a witness in the case.

The next higher command was *Heeresgruppe* C South West, which was under Field Marshal Kesselring. Above him was Adolf Hitler.

Thus, there were three commands involved in this complex process. This essentially evolved into a game of "office politics" of strict compliance and who might be "thrown under the bus," with an interpretation of Hitler's notorious *Führerbefehl*, or Commando Order, dictating the handling and disposition of captured "saboteurs."

The fifteen OGs were Italian American commandos chosen explicitly because of their military training and their ability to speak and understand the Italian language. They were all members of the US Army, wearing regulation US Army clothing and bearing US Army equipment and insignia. They were on a bona fide military mission: to demolish the railroad tunnels on the railroad line between La Spezia and Genoa. Taking down the tunnels would deprive the Germans of the ability to ship supplies and troops by rail to their forces in and around Cassino and could ultimately force a surrender of German soldiers.

Knowing they were lost and in need of food, the OGs hid out in an empty stable but were discovered the next morning, March 24, 1944. Without much of a fight, they surrendered to a small party consisting of Italian Fascist soldiers and troops of the German army.

They were trucked to La Spezia and confined in a stable near the headquarters of the 135th Fortress Brigade, Brigade Almers. (After the war, Almers was captured, detained for questioning, escaped imprisonment twice, and was never seen again. Thus, his side of the story has never been told and probably never will.)

The captured American soldiers' interrogation was performed in La Spezia by two German naval intelligence officers. During the investigation, Vincent Russo fell for a ruse by one of the officers and revealed the entire story of the mission.

On March 24, a report on the capture was made by *Oberst* Almers and telexed to the 75th Army Corps. The report immediately reached General Dostler.

The next morning, March 25, a telex was received at the headquarters of the 135th Fortress Brigade. Anton Dostler signed it. In substance it stated that "the captured Americans will be shot immediately." No due process was in place, and no trial had been scheduled.

Upon receiving the telex, *Oberst* Almers and the three naval intelligence officers resumed interrogating the OGs. It was apparent that the OGs were on a legitimate mission and should not be executed. At the very least, they believed, a stay of execution was called for; they again reached out to General Dostler. Their plea was to no avail.

Late on the afternoon of March 25, *Oberst* Almers received another telex from 75th Army Corps (Dostler) that said, in substance, that by "0700 hours tomorrow morning you would have reported compliance with the order of execution." At this point, several officers pushed back, refuting Dostler's order to sign an order for execution of the Ginny OGs.

One other officer on Dostler's staff, *Ritmeister d.r.* (Reserve Cavalry Captain) Alexander Fürst zu Dohna-Schlobitten, believed the Ginny OGs were not commandos but uniformed soldiers on a legitimate military mission who should be treated as prisoners of war.

When ordered by *Oberst* (Colonel) Horst Kraehe, Dostler's LXXV Army Corps chief of staff, to pass the execution order to *Oberst* Almers, zu Dohna refused—and almost lost his head. Instead, because he knew zu Dohna was friendly with *Reichsführer-SS* Heinrich Himmler and other influential Nazis, Dostler had zu Dohna immediately dismissed from the Army.

Oberst Almers then gave orders for conducting the execution, including assembling a firing squad and digging a grave at Punta Bianca, a desolate area on the Ligurian coast.

During the night (Saturday, March 25, to Sunday, March 26), two further attempts were made by officers of the 135th Fortress Brigade and by the naval officers conducting the interrogation to bring about a stay in the decision, telexing their request to General Dostler. All these attempts were unsuccessful, and the fifteen Americans were executed early in the morning of March 26. They were neither tried nor given any type of hearing.

No mention was made at Dostler's trial concerning the fact that the OGs had committed neither destruction nor sabotage.

[1] Kurt Mälzer, German Luftwaffe general and military commander of the city of Rome, in 1944. He commanded all Wehrmacht and SS in the city. After the Via Rasella bombing, the inebriated Mälzer wanted the entire block blown up and Rome set afire. He was found guilty of multiple war crimes. On November 30, 1946, his death sentence was commuted. He died in prison in March 1952. HISTORICAL/CORBIS HISTORICAL VIA GETTY IMAGES

[2] General Field Marshal Albert Kesselring during an intermission
in the International Military Tribunal at the Nuremberg hearings to
investigate the Supreme Command of the German Armed Forces (OKW).
HOLOCAUST MUSEUM COLLECTION

[3] View of Via Rasella, Rome, in 2015. On March 23, 1944, *Gruppi d'Azione Patriottica*, the Italian partisan group, detonated four pounds of TNT in the midst of a column of 142 marching German Police, instantly killing 33. The next day, Herbert Kappler, Gestapo chief, and Kurt Mälzer arranged for the execution of more than 300 civilians in what became known as the Ardeatine Massacre—a reprisal that has gone down as one of the worst massacres in history.

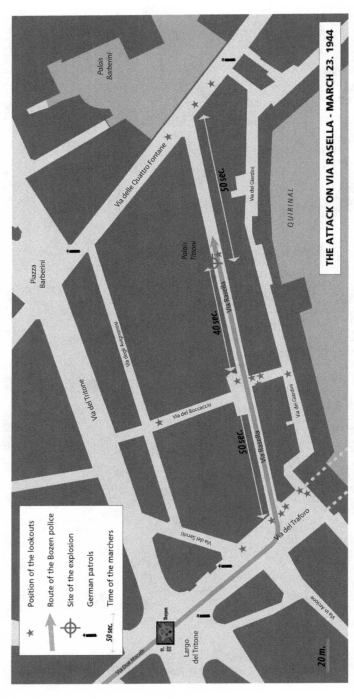

THE ATTACK ON VIA RASELLA - MARCH 23. 1944

Position of the lookouts

Route of the Bozen police

Site of the explosion

German patrols

Time of the marchers

[4] The Via Rasella area where a bomb placed by the *Gruppi d'Azione Patriottica*, or GAP, killed thirty-three German policemen marching up the street to their barracks on March 23, 1944. For years, it was erroneously suggested that the police were SS. They were not; they were German Order Police. The bomb exploded where the car and man are at the top of the photo.
EMANUELE MASTRANGELO/CC ATTRIBUTION-SHAR ALIKE 4.0

[5] *General der Infanterie* (Lieutenant General) Anton Dostler, who was found guilty of ordering the execution of the fifteen members of the US Army's Operation Ginny, being roped to a stake and receiving Last Rites from an American and a German chaplain prior to his execution on December 1, 1945. ***Note:*** His gorgets and sovereign eagle, swastika, and awards have been removed.

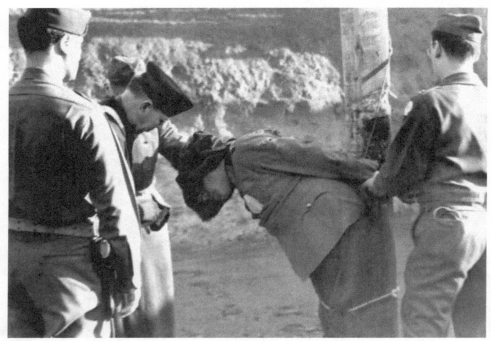

[6] General Dostler, at 0911 hours on December 1, 1945, in Aversa, Italy, slumped over after he was executed by fifteen US Army sharpshooters. Considerable damage can be seen to the back of his tunic. He was the first and last German officer executed by firing squad.
KEYSTONE-FRANCE/GAMMA-KEYSTONE VIA GETTY IMAGES

[7] SS Gestapo Chief *SS-Obersturmbannführer* Herbert Kappler, a critical German functionary in Rome and a war criminal during the Nazi era, after his arrest. Serving as head of
German police and security services (*Sicherheitspolizei und SD*) in Rome, he organized and
supervised the Ardeatine massacre with Kurt Mälzer. On a visit in August 1977, Kappler's
wife carried him out in a large suitcase (Kappler weighed about 104 lbs. at the time) and
escaped to West Germany. Kappler died at home in Soltau, on February 9, 1978, aged 70.
HISTORICAL/CORBIS HISTORICAL VIA GETTY IMAGES

[8] Site of the Ardeatine massacre (*Eccidio delle Fosse Ardeatine*) near the Appian Way, Rome. Here occurred the mass killing of 335 civilians and political prisoners on March 24, 1944, by Kappler's SS. The killings were in reprisal for the Via Rasella attack in central Rome the previous day against SS Police Regiment *Bozen*. The victims were brought into the cave to tunnels and killed, one at a time, each with one shot to the back of the head; it took almost all day and night. ANTMOOSE: FLICKR

CHAPTER 8

Dostler Surrenders

THE 85TH INFANTRY DIVISION (CD) IS DISTINGUISHED IN AMERICAN military history.

During WWII, three soldiers from the division won the Medal of Honor. In Belluno-Agordo, Italy, the Division cleaned up fleeing German troops until their mass surrender on May 2, 1945. The Division is also known as the "Custer Division" (named for cavalry commander George Armstrong Custer), hence the "CD" on its shoulder patch. The Division currently exists as the 85th Support Command.

On May 3, 1945, the 85th Infantry Division achieved another distinction: It accepted General Anton Dostler's peaceful surrender at Calazzo, Italy, west of Genoa.

Three days later, officers of the OSS Secret Intelligence Group discovered Dostler's involvement in the execution of the Ginny OGs. Dostler freely admitted that the American soldiers, dressed in regulation US Army uniforms, had landed somewhere near Bonassola in March 1944 and were "summarily shot without a trial in accordance with the order of the Führer" and that he, Dostler, did not "personally wish to make a decision as to whether that very severe Führer Order should be carried out." This was a lie; he had far more concern for his career as a general—and his life—than showing compassion for the Ginny OGs. At the very least, his admission shows his complicity in the matter of execution.

Dostler had quickly presented his indecisiveness regarding the execution order to his Army Group leader, *General der Infanterie* (General of the Infantry) Gustav-Adolf Karl Friedrich Ernst von Zangen, Commanding General, LXXXVII Corps.

Von Zangen's headquarters replied "yes," giving the go-ahead order for killing the OGs. Now, von Zangen was implicated. As a result of headquarters' response, Dostler passed along the order to carry out the executions to Brigade Almers's commanding officer. He must have felt a load taken off his shoulders because, he believed, it had been von Zangen, not he, who had *initiated* the order. Dostler repeatedly stated that he did not *originate* the order but that "it came from Gustov [*sic*] von Zangen." And, he said, he was being faithful to the Commando Order and the oath he had taken in 1933 when Hitler and the Nazi government took office.

While in their custody, Dostler told the Americans that he passed von Zangen's order to have the Ginny OGs executed to *Oberst* (Colonel) Kurt Almers's 135 Brigade (Brigade Almers), whose command was immediately responsible for holding the Ginny OGs. Dostler told his interrogators that "he was working in compliance with the Hitler Order, the *Führerbefehl*, aka the Commando Order, that all persons while engaging in sabotage would be executed." Because he had received the order to go ahead with the execution from von Zangen, Dostler believed there was a big difference between *initiating* and *passing along* an order—a point he took with him to trial.

On July 19, 1944, in his second report, Lieutenant Blythin attached a sworn statement by von Zangen in which he, von Zangen, claimed to have no knowledge of the events of March 24–25. This is Blythin's report containing von Zangen's statement:

I. According to the statement of Gen. Dostler, it seems that [:]

    a. [General Dostler] had forwarded the inquiries of Brigade Almers through his Chief [of Staff], "Oberst" Kraehe, to the Chief of Staff of the "*Armeegruppe* v. Zangen," "Oberst" Nagel, at present [*Generalmajor* Nagel].

    b. That [Dostler] had been waiting for this decision for a longer period of time [,] and that he reminded [his chief of this] several times.

    c. That his chief had informed him [,] probably based on consultation with the "*Armeegruppe*" (Higher Commando [,] that the "*Armeegruppe*" had not yet received the decision [from] the "*Heeresgruppe*."

    d. [...]

e. That finally, when the order that the *"Führerbefehl"* had to be carried, arrived, at about 5 o'clock in the afternoon [25 Mar 44], [Dostler] ordered the execution to take place next morning at 7 o'clock.

II. *All this indicated that Gen. Dostler ordered the execution on the command of a superior authority* [emphasis added]. That the authority in question must have been either the *"Heeresgruppe,"* or the High Command (OKW, and not the *"Armeegruppe"*) and that the latter only forwarded the decision—probably in my absence—to Gen. Dostler, may be concluded from the following:

a. After one and a quarter years, I myself can only remember a limited number of sabotage attempts from that time; however, I cannot recall details or cases of special importance. Often, these proved to be false [alarms]; once our own patrol destroyed a small boat along the coast, in which, it seemed, two or three people had landed. I remember, however, a report about an unsuccessful attempt against a tunnel, in or near La Spezia. But I cannot tell without first speaking to my Chief of that time, Gen. Nagel, whether that attempt is identical with the one under investigation now.

b. Owing to the extraordinary and large area under my command (the Ligurian coast from the Italian, French frontiers to Elba, the Adriatic coast from south of Ancona to Fiume, the Apennines, important territories in the rear of the army, with all large towns of Northern Italy and Austria), I spent more time on inspection tours, often several days and nights, than with the battle Headquarters of the *"Armeegruppe."* In my absence, the Chief of Staff had full authority in all current matters, general or otherwise important[,] questions[,] were left for my decision, upon my return, or forwarded to the superior *"Heeresgruppe* to the *"Heersgruppe* headquarters" which was superior to us[.] General Nagel acknowledged this arrangement, and upon my return, he generally informed me of the most important events. The fact that General Nagel, following the inquires of "Oberst" Kraehe by phone, submitted the case in question to the "*Heeresgruppe*" for decision, is evident from the statement under Ie, which Dostler seems to remember too.

b. There are no diaries, or other notes at my disposal which would enable me to establish the place where I had been at the time. Also no notes about important telephone conversation, which would give valuable information pertaining to this case [are] available. They formed part of the war diaries that had been destroyed by air attacks in Germany. However, even without such notes I have to assume that at the time Gen. Dostler made his inquiries I could not be reached. This is evident—with reservation, until the confirmation of Gen. Nagel—from the following:

1. I would undoubtedly remember after such a long time, and in spite of the strenuous events in other theaters of the war, if the inquiries [from Headquarters, 75th Army Corps] had been presented to me, I would have asked for the exact wording of the [Commando Order], would have examined the state of the affair[,] and then only would I have made a decision myself, or ordered that a decision be made. In no way can I remember such procedure.

2. From the above[-]mentioned plot against a tunnel in, or at La Spezia which I am [un]able to recall, I conclude that I might have arrived only after the completion of the case. The fact that I do not remember details from the official [report] of the case, which in all probability took place as [usual], might be due to the long time that passed since then, and also the fact the completed matter had not been reported in all details. Otherwise I would [be] bound to remember details, such as: "members of the American Army, Army uniforms, 15-man strong." But that is not the case. I have heard for the first time, during my interrogation [,] that there had appeared

Americans along my coast, where at that time we only counted on the presence of the English, or sometimes Italians. Furthermore it is my honest conviction that during the whole war, at several posts of duty in all theaters of war, I myself had never pronounced a death sentence against a soldier of the enemy, nor against a civilian. Therefore, it is simply impossible that I should not remember the shooting of fifteen men, especially members of the American army, wearing uniforms, had it taken place on my own [order], or the order of a member of my Staff.

3. Furthermore, my absence seems to me to be proved by the fact that Gen. Dostler, contrary to our habits, had not called me by phone to ask me to intervene, after his Chief had failed to obtain the proposed decision. Gen. Dostler noticed this fact too, during our talk on June 25 [1945]. He stated that we usually cleared existing doubts by telephone conversations.

III. For further clearance in this matter, I find it absolutely [essential] that [Brigadier General] Nagel, as well as "Oberst" Krahe [*sic*], be interrogated. Furthermore, it seems to me that it is of first importance: to obtain a copy of the "*Füh rerbefehl.*" It should be present among the documents of the High Command (OKW or OKH), if only those [who were] originally responsible did not destroy everything pertaining to this matter. [This severe decree differentiated] between several groups of persons, and covered in the most severe form that the procedure applied against certain groups be strictly according to the above decree, leaving no other possibilities, and threatened all members of the German army who acted differently with Court-Martial.

So, we ask, who was lying—Dostler or von Zangen? Or both? Dostler said he received an emphatic "yes" from von Zangen when asked about the execution order. Von Zangen said no such thing happened, and in his statement, *"All this indicated that Gen. Dostler ordered the execution on the command of a superior authority* [emphasis added]. That the authority in question must have been either the *Heeresgruppe* or the High Command (OKW, and not the *Armeegruppe*."* Lieutenant Blythin later concluded that the liar here was Dostler, anxious to cover himself, to get on with the executions and then shift the responsibility of following an official order onto his higher command, von Zangen. Later, Blythin let von Zangen off the hook when he wrote that von Zangen's statement was truthful: "There is no direct evidence of his (von Zangen's) participation in the matter, and it is thought that on the basis of evidence in hand [he] could not be held as a defendant. He is in custody pending further investigation."

Dostler, as we have seen through the eyes of von Zangen, was unwilling to order the executions until he heard from *Oberst* (Colonel) Horst Kraehe, until he had received confirmation from Headquarters LXXV. Essentially, Dostler was looking for authorization from above—and if he couldn't get it, he'd lie about it.

Von Zangen claimed he was not at his headquarters, so Col. Walter Nagel, von Zangen's chief of staff, relayed Dostler's request upward to the *Heeresgruppe* (Army Group).

It should be noted that in the German Army, it was the chiefs of staff who spoke to one another. This could mean that Nagel spoke with *Generalmajor* (Major General) Siegfried Carl Theodor Westphal, Kesselring's Chief of the General Staff of *Heeresgruppe C*, located at Monte Soratte. But this is questionable: Why would Westphal, on his own initiative, authorize the execution of the Ginny OGs? Highly unlikely for a major general.

According to von Zangen, when authentication of the executions arrived at his headquarters on March 25, "Dostler had ordered that the executions be carried out at 0700 hours the next morning." However, at Dostler's trial, von Zangen lied about when he heard about the executions, swearing that "[he had heard for the first time in June 1945, while a POW] that American soldiers were alleged to have been shot in [his] area."

Two officers in the chain of command knew precisely who was involved and exactly how the execution order proceeded to the point of implementation: *Oberst* (Colonel) Horst Kraehe and *Generalmajor* (Major General) Walter Nagel. Dostler knew this, knew their testimony could improve his case and perhaps save his life. He petitioned the Commission, asking that these two officers be brought in to testify regarding this crucial point.

Had these men testified, Dostler's fate could have been favorable. However, as luck would have it, Kraehe had disappeared and was never apprehended. Walter Nagel was at a POW camp in Italy but had been misidentified and then he escaped, never to be seen again. Unfortunately for Dostler, they never had an opportunity to testify.

The commander of the Ginny firing squad, *Hauptmann* (Captain) Wilhelm Rehfeld, *was* in custody; however, somehow he was not identified as the much-sought-after *Hauptmann* Wilhelm Rehfeld and was not charged. Thus, the officer who actually ordered the riflemen to fire also escaped Allied justice.

On June 11, 1945, a sworn statement was signed by Anton Dostler, which, you can see from his perspective, confirms receiving the "yes" regarding the execution of the Ginny OGs:

I, the undersigned, General of the Infantry, DOSTLER, Anton, hereby declare that in the spring of 1944, I was in command of the 75th Corps which was detailed to the coast defense from the Ventimiglia sector [to] south of Livorno. The 135th Fortress Brigade under the command of Colonel Almers was deployed on both sides of La Spezia in the sector of this Corps. One day it was reported from the Fortress Brigade that soldiers from a sabotage unit composed of American soldiers[,] which had the assignment of blowing up a railroad tunnel[,] had been captured. There existed a very strict order from the Füehrer[,] the number and date of which I can no longer remember[,] according to which *it was forbidden to take enemy sabotage troops prisoner. They had to be entirely annihilated in such a manner that no evidence would remain* [emphasis added]. I forwarded the report[,] which had been received[,] to Army Headquarters with a request for decision as to whether this order of the Füehrer should be carried out also in this instance. The Army Headquarters ordered that the saboteurs were to be shot. The answer was given either by the Chief of Staff, Colonel Nagel, or by the General of the Infantry von Zangen himself. I forwarded the order to Colonel Almers of the 135 Fortress Brigade for execution. I remember having heard that Army Headquarters had submitted the matter to Army Group Southwest C for decision.

Like von Zangen later, Dostler, in the above sworn statement, seems certain that Kesselring was the "higher authority" who had authorized the Ginny executions and passed his order down the chain of command.

Von Zangen clearly remembered the incident of the fifteen OGs and that *Oberst* Almers had passed this information on to Dostler, and that Dostler had then passed this along to Army Group von Zangen. "Army," he said, "ordered that the prisoners be executed in accordance with Hitler's Commando Order." It was Colonel Kraehe, Dostler's chief of staff, who received this order from above. But did Kraehe speak directly with von Zangen or with Colonel Nagel, the latter's chief of staff, if von Zangen had been absent?

On July 19, 1945, Lieutenant Blythin recommended that if Almers continued to elude apprehension, the trial against Dostler should move forward. The assembled evidence of the Dostler file at this point was passed along to the Office of the Judge Advocate General (JAG) in Washington, DC, for review and evaluation.

JAG Capt. Anthony Kosac filed a summary on August 29, 1945. In part, it stated:

A German Navy company commanded by Captain DeSuti was identified [incorrectly] as the unit which carried out the Ginny execution, "although later reports indicated the execution detail was commanded by Hauptmann Rehfeld." Captain Kosac mentioned the "crushed condition of the heads of the victims" but added that these could have resulted from [coup de grâce] shots to the back of the head which witness Knell testified he had seen. General Dostler ordered the execution "on the command of higher authority," and his trial was scheduled to proceed "whether or not Colonel Almers is found."

Those familiar with the case were not surprised with the verdict, which was issued by General Richmond, Theater Judge Advocate, Mediterranean Theater of Operations, USA. The charge was a violation of the "law of war" with a single specification: "Contrary to the law of war," it was alleged that the defendant "ordered fifteen members of the Army of the United States, then recently captured, to be shot summarily, which order was carried into execution on or about 26 March 1944, resulting in their deaths."

Dostler would now be judged and sentenced for committing a war crime.

CHAPTER 9

Duty to Obey

THE PALAZZO DI GIUSTIZIA (PALACE OF JUSTICE) IN ROME, COLLOQUI-
ally referred to among Italians as Il Palazzaccio (the Bad Palace), is the
seat of the Supreme Court of Cassation and the Judicial Public Library.
The massive building with the imposing title, grand and ornate, is located
in the Prati district. Above the facade looking toward the River Tiber, is a
great bronze quadriga, set there in 1926, the work of the sculptor Ettore
Ximenes from Palermo. Ten giant statues of notable jurists adorn the
ramps before the main facade and the interior courtyard. The upper part
of the facade looking onto the Piazza Cavour is ornamented with a bronze
coat of arms of the House of Savoy. Inside the Hall of the Supreme Court,
also known as the Great Hall, are several intricate frescoes. Designed by
Perugia architect Guglielmo Calderini and built between 1888 and 1910,
the Palace of Justice was considered one of the grandest of the new buildings constructed following proclamation of Rome as the capital of the
Kingdom of Italy.

On October 8, 1945, a Sunday, at 1000 hours, Anton Dostler's trial
commenced in this ornate building.

Between the time of Dostler's capture on May 3, 1945, until this Sunday, several considerations had come up before the Commission that had
the potential to save him from execution. They were either disregarded or
considered inapplicable to his case.

Those considerations started with his legal team, specifically a young
defense lawyer, Cecil Kent Emery, who had graduated from law school
in the mid-1930s. Through his school's ROTC program, he was commissioned as a second lieutenant when he graduated. On the day of the
attack on Pearl Harbor, December 7, 1941, Emery received a phone call
summoning him to serve as an officer in the US Army. At the time, he

was thirty-seven years old, an advanced age to be going into the Army, but because he had graduated from ROTC and was a lawyer, the Army saw a need for his skills. He served with the Second Division of the US Cavalry, which saw action in the North Africa campaign, until they reached Rome. He then wound up with the troops of the Fifth Army. He was transferred to the Judge Advocate General's office. Soon after, Emery, now a major, was appointed one of Anton Dostler's counsels alongside lead counsel Colonel Wolfe. This was a historic moment for Emery and everyone involved in the case because it was the first Allied war crimes trial following WWII. All knew, for better or worse, that it would establish multiple precedents for the upcoming Nuremberg Trials, which would begin on November 20, 1945.

Both Wolfe and Emery knew the charges so far, but they felt sure there were several weaknesses in the case against Dostler. They also felt strongly that, according to the standard rules of evidence and the Code of Conduct, the charges against Dostler should be dropped.

However, back in Washington, DC, the Truman administration had been telling the American people for months that "not a single German officer guilty of war crimes would be set free." After all this posturing, if the first German officer tried for war crimes was acquitted and released, it would be a major embarrassment for President Harry Truman and his administration.

Wolfe and Emery sent a telex to Washington outlining their position, citing the scarcity of solid evidence, much hearsay, and lack of witnesses to support their case. Shortly after, they received a stunning response: "Lacking standard evidence, hearsay will be accepted as evidence in the trial." This decision established another precedent for the upcoming Nuremberg Trials.

After Dostler pled not guilty to the charge and specification, the judge advocate presented a clumsy argument filled with myriad technical errors. The judge advocate, Maj. Frederick W. Roche, was obviously not familiar with German military terminology in a case where a man's life was at stake. For example, referring to the several German headquarters involved, he said, "[Dostler's next higher headquarters above the 75th Army Corps was called Army Corps Von Zaengen [*sic*], and "[I]n the early afternoon of

March 25, Colonel Almers called the 75th Army Group and had a conversation, most of which will be in evidence."These mistakes and others could have been easily avoided if Roche had consulted with Allied officers who were thoroughly familiar with the English translations.

A US Army captain, A. R. Materazzi, was the prosecution's first witness. He provided the court with a brief overview of Ginny II, emphasizing that the OGs were in US Army uniforms and that Ginny was a military mission. Both points were vital because they showed that the OGs should not have been mistaken for Partisans, and that their presence behind enemy lines conformed with international law. A roster of Unit A, First Contingent, dated May 19, 1944, included their names, proving that the Ginny OGs were soldiers of the US Army and, if captured, eligible for protection under international law.

Unlike the Nuremberg Trials, where the strategy to convict was founded mostly on piles of documentation, the prosecution at Dostler's trial believed testimony from multiple witnesses would be enough to convict him. After the formal aspects of its prima facie case, the prosecution addressed events that had preceded the executions:

The first person who had seen the OGs at Corozzo was witness German *Oberstleutnant* (First Lieutenant) Georg Schultz, an ordnance officer on Almers's staff. He testified that he had seen the execution order telexed from the 75th Army Corps sometime after it had arrived at staff headquarters of Fortress Brigade Almers, at around 1000 hours, March 25. He could not remember if the sender had been General Dostler or Colonel Kraehe.

Rudolph Bolze told the court how he had responded to Colonel Almers's order to organize the excavation site for the OGs' grave on Punta Bianca peninsula and said that he was subsequently in the vicinity of the executions and had witnessed the shooting and subsequent burial of the corpses.

No witness, however, knew of any judicial proceeding that had afforded the OGs the right of due process. In other words, the OGs had received no formal hearing or trial.

Not once before or during the trial did Dostler deny that he had ordered the executions. Because of this, Dostler's lawyers felt it would be absurd to enter a plea of not guilty. But they saw several significant cracks in the prosecution's case:

1. It had long been a tradition of German soldiers to obey without question orders from their superiors, orders from heads of state. This had been initially prescribed in the soldier's oath (*Fahnen-eid*), which Dostler and all German soldiers had sworn to Hitler in August 1934. Colonel Wolfe argued that this left the accused with no other choice than to obey his oath to Hitler and order the execution of the Ginny OGs. A copy of the Commando Order, captured in France in December 1944, was introduced into evidence by the prosecution. However, Dostler said, a Supplement to that order had been issued by Hitler, defining who should be considered a saboteur and/or a commando, for whom execution was mandatory. Dostler had studiously read the order before ordering the executions. It would, he claimed, show that he was obeying the order written by Hitler in the Supplement.

2. The defendant, Dostler, had given the final order for executions of those for whom executions were mandatory only after he had requested and received proper authorization from a higher authority. This higher authority was at least equally responsible for the war crime, the murder of the fifteen Ginny OGs. Dostler considered himself bound to obey the *Führerbefehl* and its Supplement. This was brought out by Colonel Wolfe, Dostler's lead counselor:

Colonel Wolfe: Will you please state as near as you can the substance of the oath [to Hitler] that you took in [August 1934]?

Dostler: I don't know exactly the text but know that it contained absolute faith and absolute obedience to Füehrer and Fatherland.

Colonel Wolfe: Under the oath, did you understand that it was mandatory that you obey all orders received from the Füehrer or under his authority?

Dostler: Yes.

Colonel Wolfe:	What would be the effect [on an officer if he disobeyed] an order of the Füehrer, or of a superior authority in the German Army [after he had taken this oath of allegiance?]
Dostler:	He could come before a courts-martial [*sic*].
Colonel Wolfe:	Was that the same understanding of your oath and all requirements to obey orders as existed in March 1944?
Dostler:	Yes.
Colonel Wolfe:	Will you state to the Commission if you know whether there is any provisions in German military law or German law which would authorize an officer to disobey an order of superior military authorities?
Dostler:	We [had] to execute all orders.

Corroboration of this testimony came from former German general Fridolin von Senger und Etterlin, a witness for the defense:

Colonel Wolfe:	During your time of service and of General Dostler's service, were Army officers required to take oaths of allegiance in the German Army?
Senger:	They were.
Colonel Wolfe:	What was the last date that officers in the German Army were required to take oaths of allegiance?
Senger:	We were required to take a new oath when the National Socialist government came into power, so that must have been in 1933.
Colonel Wolfe:	1933?
Senger:	[In August 1933], we took a new oath, the wording of which I don't remember exactly.
Colonel Wolfe:	Could you state to the court the substance of that oath?
Senger:	The substance, as far as I remember, the wording of the oath was very short, and it contained practically only

the impression of loyalty and strict [obedience] to the Füehrer, Adolf Hitler himself.

Colonel Wolfe: Is that the same oath that General Dostler was also required to take?

Senger: I am sure.

Colonel Wolfe: Did that oath that you took allow or permit disobedience of any orders issued by Hitler or under his authority?

Senger: It did not.

Colonel Wolfe: What would be the penalty for disobedience of such orders?

Senger: The penalties were determined in our penal law. That the penalty in the case of war became more severe, as many generals [were] punished for [disobeying orders. This] occurred especially in the last year, [when] leaders took decisions on their own and were punished afterward because the High Command [was] of the opinion that they were not entitled to do so.

Colonel Wolfe: Then I understand that punishment was given not only for disobedience of orders but also for errors made in tactical decisions, is that your testimony?

Senger: [At this stage of the war[,] with the contact by wireless and other telegraphic means [always available,] any general could communicate any decision he was to take to the Supreme Command, so we were always in close contact with the Supreme Command; however, it happened now and then that one of them [was] forced to take a decision upon his own because the situation was urgent, and I know of cases where officers were prosecuted even for those decisions on the ground of having been disobedient.

Colonel Wolfe: Are you familiar with any provision in German military penal law as it existed at that time which made it legal to disobey an order of higher command?

Senger: I don't believe there were.

Colonel Wolfe: Based on your knowledge of the German Army and its penal law, is illegality of an order a defense for disobedience of that order in the German Army?

Senger: It was not.

Major Frederick W. Roche, the judge advocate / prosecutor, asked Dostler if his oath obliged him to obey every *Führerbefehl*:

Major Roche: Can you cite to this Commission a single case of a general officer in the German Army who was executed for disobedience of an order?

Dostler: I have heard of two cases, one of which I know; the second one is only a rumor.

Major Roche: Do you know of a single case in the German Army in which a general officer was executed for disobedience of the [*Führerbefehl*] [*sic*] which has been introduced in evidence in this case (handing prosecution Exhibit No. 1 to the witness)?

Senger: This one?

Major Roche: This particular [*Führerbefehl*].

Senger: No, I didn't.

Major Roche: Do you consider that the oath which you and the accused took in [1934] bound you to obedience of an order which was none the less in violation of well-established principles of international law?

Senger: There was never any discussion on this question nor any decision put upon us, so we never considered the question [and were certain that] the question of

	international law was complied with by the government[,] not by the single officer who had to execute orders.
Major Roche:	Are you familiar with the general principle of international law regarding the treatment of prisoners of war?
Senger:	I am.
Major Roche:	Do you know that [according to] international law that they are not to be summarily executed?
Senger:	I know it.
Major Roche:	Do you consider that the oath you took in [1934] would bind you to obedience of an order by the Füehrer to execute prisoners of war summarily?
Senger:	I am convinced that as the things were that the Füehrer gave out orders which in some way interfered with the international laws, but we on the front who had to execute these orders were on the other hand convinced that in those cases he would [have made a statement or by some means informed the enemy] governments of his decisions, so that we were not responsible for the carrying out of his orders.
Major Roche:	Was there any [regulation] which prevented you from resigning from the German Army so as not to take this oath to the Füehrer?
Senger:	I am not sure whether [this held true in 1933/34,] but I am sure that in some cases later on the increasing demand [for] officers [occasioned] by the increase of the Army later had the consequence that no officer, as it was before, could retire [for personal reasons, but was required] to certify that either he was not fit physically or [for] other reasons or [was] not fit to fulfill his post; so it was in time of war.
Major Roche:	You don't know of a single instance in the German Army wherein a general officer was executed for failing

to carry out the provision of this [Commando Order] which is in evidence?

Senger: No, I don't.

Von Senger assumed that Hitler had formally informed Allied governments before he had issued an order such as the *Führerbefehl* and its Supplement, even though he probably knew they were unlawful. This was dictated by international law. Because of this, von Senger believed that Hitler's subordinates should not be held accountable for obeying Hitler's illegal orders. Von Senger was a reputable witness, honest and not a "Nazi general." A Rhodes Scholar and an orthodox Catholic, he was never accused of a war crime; war crimes were abhorrent to him. In fact, he had successfully disobeyed a criminal order from Hitler to execute Italians without suffering punishment, although the reason is unknown.

The defense argued that Dostler had read the Supplement before he issued the execution order. Dostler had also read the Commando Order, and these two documents had assured him that the order to execute the OGs was both valid and legal:

Colonel Wolfe: General Dostler, you have heard read into evidence what is known as the *Führerbefehl* of October 18, 1942. Will you please state to the commission whether you were familiar with that in March 1944?

Dostler: Yes, I knew the Füehrer Order ever since it was issued. I had seen it at the time of its issue in Russia.

Colonel Wolfe: This is a copy of the *Führerbefehl* of 1942 as it was valid in March 1944. In the order that laid on my desk in March 1944 it was much more in detail. I don't recall whether it was that order and a Supplement to it or whether that order and a Supplement had been combined. In any case the *Führerbefehl* which was laying [*sic*] in front of me listed the various categories of operation which may come under the *Führerbefehl*. In addition, there was something said in the *Führerbefehl* about the interrogation of men belonging to sabotage troops and shooting of these men after their interrogation.

Colonel Wolfe: General Dostler, was this *Führerbefehl* which you now have in your hand substantially as it existed in 1942?

Dostler: Yes.

Colonel Wolfe: Was that later supplemented by a Supplement or was a new one issued?

Dostler: I stated that I am not quite clear about the point, whether a new *Führerbefehl* covering the whole matter came out or whether only a Supplement came out and the former *Führerbefehl* was still in existence.

Colonel Wolfe: Did the new *Führerbefehl* which you had in 1944 contain substantially everything that was in the one of 1942?

Dostler: Yes, it contained that and in addition specific additions and instructions.

Colonel Wolfe: Now, will you please state, in order to clear this up, were there any additional instructions with reference to saboteurs and what constituted a saboteur?

Dostler The *Führerbefehl* has as its subject commando operations[;] there is a list of what is to be construed as [a] commando operation. I know exactly that a mission to explode something, to blow up something, came under the concept of commando troops.

Colonel Wolfe: Will you state to the commission how the *Führerbefehl* came into you possession?

Dostler: The *Führerbefehl* came to me through the channels from the Army Group.

Colonel Wolfe: Do you know who issued the *Führerbefehl*?

Dostler: The Supreme Command of the Wehrmacht.

Colonel Wolfe: Were you required as an Army officer to comply with this *Führerbefehl?*

Dostler: Yes.

Colonel Wolfe: If you know[,] what would be the penalty for disobeying the *Führerbefehl?*

Dostler: I don't know exactly what the penalty would be but I knew only that a [court-]martial was expressly threatened in the *Führerbefehl* in the case of disobedience to it.

Here are relevant passages from the Commando Order of October 18, 1942:

1. [In the first paragraph Hitler claimed a captured order revealed the British intended to shackle and kill German POWs under certain conditions. Other orders were found "in which the killing of prisoners has never been required as standard practice."]

2. For this reason it has already been announced in an addendum to the [OKW communiqué] of October 7, 1942, that in the future, Germany[,] in the face of these sabotage troops of the British and their accomplices, will resort to the same procedure, i.e., that [captured soldiers] will be ruthlessly mowed down by the German troops in combat, where they may appear.

3. I therefore order: From now on all enemies on so-called commando missions in Europe or Africa challenged by German troops, whether armed or unarmed, in battle or in flight, are to be slaughtered to the last man. It does not make any difference whether they are landed from ships or aeroplane for the actions, whether they are dropped by parachute. Even if these individuals when found, should apparently be prepared to give themselves up, as a matter of principle, no pardon is to be granted them. In each individual case full information is to be sent to the OKW for publication in the armed forces communiqué.

4. If individual members of such commandos, such as agents, saboteurs, etc., fall into the hands of the military forces by some other

means, through the police in occupied territories for instance, they are to be handed over immediately to the Security Service. Any imprisonment under military guard, in PW stockades for instance, etc., is strictly prohibited, even if this is only intended for a short time.

5. I will hold responsible under military law, for failing to carry out this order, all commanders and officers who either have neglected their duty of instructing troops about his order, or acted against this order where it was to be executed.

The *Führerbefehl* was distributed to twenty-three addresses. Attached was a note saying, "This order is not to be distributed beyond the battalion and equivalent staff of the other branches of the armed forces. After having been noted, *copies distributed beyond the regiments* and the equivalent staffs of the other branches of the armed forces *are to be collected and destroyed.*" [All italics are as in the original.]

Today, in reading over this, there is clearly nothing ambiguous about the document: "Enemy soldiers who were captured behind the lines, in uniform or not, were defined as a commando/saboteur 'and were to be annihilated.'"

For Dostler, there were no other alternatives. He was complying with an order submitted to him by his Supreme Commander, Adolf Hitler (and if disobeyed would have resulted in his court-martial and possible execution).

Lieutenant Blythin assessed the evidence of the case against Dostler and, on September 14, 1945, sent an overview to Brigadier General Richmond, Judge Advocate General of the Mediterranean Theater USA.

General Richmond's reply was nothing short of brilliant. He flipped the case over on its head, but he would receive scant recognition for his new perspective. "The point of this case," Richmond replied, "is not who issued the order that commandos would be summarily shot as set forth in the *Führerbefehl* but rather whether the [A]mericans came within the provisions of the order."

Today it can be categorically stated that the Ginny OGs did fall within the provisions of the Commando Order.

But Dostler's defense team was not obligated to heed Richmond's opinion. In fact, it was disregarded. Had the opinion been studied before Dostler's trial and presented as part of the defense, might have been found not guilty.

Further confusing the matter, Dostler could have been court-martialed by the German government because he did not immediately turn the Ginny OGs over to the *Sicherheitsdienst des Reichsführers-SS* (Security Service of the Reichsführer-SS, or SD); this was demanded by the Commando Order. The SD would have trucked them off and had them immediately executed.

The Americans, it seems, were pushing the case in the direction they wanted: a death sentence for General Dostler and full compliance with the administration's public intent to severely punish every German officer guilty of a war crime. However, many Americans felt that American justice was not being served in Dostler's trial.

General Dostler, through his own words and those of others around him, said he was following the orders of a higher authority and passed along that order to execute the fifteen OGs to Colonel Almers. He was merely adhering to what would become known as the "Nuremberg Defense," or "just following orders." Essentially, this plea claims that a person, whether a member of the military, law enforcement, or the civilian population, should not be considered guilty of committing actions ordered by a superior officer.

This defense had been used successfully multiple times in the past and was first presented on June 4, 1921, when the legal doctrine of superior orders was used during the German Military Trials conducted after World War I.

One of the most famous of these trials was that of Lt. Karl Neumann, a U-boat captain responsible for sinking the HMHS (His Majesty's Hospital Ship) *Dover Castle*. On May 26, 1917, the *Dover Castle* was torpedoed fifty nautical miles north of Bône, Algeria, by *UC-67*; fourteen lives were lost. Neumann admitted to having sunk the ship and stated that he had done so obeying orders from the German Admiralty and so could not be held liable for his actions. The *Reichsgericht* (Germany's Supreme Court) acquitted Neumann, accepting the defense of superior orders to allow him to escape criminal liability. Further, the court stated, "all civilized nations recognize the principle that a subordinate is covered by the orders of his superiors."

Many accused of war crimes during World War I were acquitted using a similar defense, creating immense dissatisfaction among the Allies.

The Dostler case is thought to be one of the main causes for removal of this defense in the August 8, 1945, London Charter of the International Military Tribunal. The removal was initiated by Robert H. Jackson, an associate justice of the US Supreme Court, and the chief prosecutor at the Nuremberg Trials.

During those trials, for example, Field Marshal Wilhelm Keitel, *Oberkommando der Wehrmacht* (OKW); Field Marshall Alfred Jodl, Chief of the Operations Staff of the Wehrmacht, the German Armed Forces High Command; and other Nazi defendants unsuccessfully advanced the "superior orders" defense. They often stated that while they knew that many of Adolf Hitler's orders were unlawful, or at least had reason to believe they were unlawful, their place was not to question the illegality but to obey the order. Using the "Nuremberg defense," they claimed they were "only following orders" (*"Befehl ist Befehl"*; "an order is an order") and so were not responsible for their crimes. They claimed they were compelled to do so by the *Führerprinzip* (Leader Principle) that governed the entire Nazi regime, as well as their own oath of allegiance to Hitler. In most cases, the tribunal found the defendants' offenses so egregious that obedience to superior orders could not be considered a mitigating factor.

In preparing his closing remarks, Colonel Wolfe appeared to show that *Generalfeldmarschall* (General Field Marshal) Kesselring had almost certainly confirmed Dostler's order to proceed with the executions, which Dostler obediently did. As Dostler stated numerous times, he had not *originated* the order from Almers to prepare for the execution—instead he had *passed along* the order he received from Army Group von Zangen (which Zangen denied).

However, Wolfe erred in his remarks when he cited a paragraph from *The Rules of Land Warfare*, edition October 1940, which he read for the Commission. The paragraph stated that *"enemy soldiers were not to be punished for war crimes when the action had been sanctioned by a superior officer or his government"* [emphasis added]. He was apparently unaware that this passage had been revised in November 1944 to counter the "obedience to superior orders" defense that many saw coming in the Nuremberg war crimes trials. Yet he found significance in a soldier's duty to obey when he said to the Commission, "This time we won the war; next time we might not win it. Next time you gentlemen might be sitting [in the defendant's chair] and the victorious enemy might be sitting [where you are now]."

Wolfe hoped the evidence he presented would result in only imprisonment for Dostler—not execution.

Dostler added that key elements were missing from his defense. His defense noted: "Key witnesses that he had requested were unaccounted for. And the other, that it was his duty to obey orders and he obeyed them. He felt that it was not *his* order that caused this unfortunate incident, but that it was the order of a higher headquarters and that [he] acted only for them and at their direction. As such, he requests that his sentence be reduced to imprisonment; or, that his execution be suspended until the missing witnesses be found and could give their evidence."

It was not to be. The Commission found no mitigating circumstances in the matter.

At 1600 hours, October 11, the commission retired to deliberate Dostler's fate. The next day, at 0900 hours, the president announced that the Commission had found Dostler guilty of the charge and specification.

They sentenced him to be "shot to death by musketry," an odd, antique of a word from the French *mousquetaire*, dating back to 1640–1650, meaning "the technique of bringing fire from a group of rifle and automatic weapons to bear on specified targets."

Many US Army officers in the gallery gasped when they heard the sentence. To many, it meant that a general could lose his life for obeying an order when the result was determined to be a war crime. Some were not happy with the result. A sense of injustice wafted thought the courtroom.

On October 24 Dostler filed a petition listing several reasons he believed the evidence should be further reexamined. Among the items on his list was the absence of the Supplement to Hitler's *Kommandobefehl*, which, he claimed, had been extremely important in validating his decision to pass along the order to execute the OGs. Sessler and Klaps had not been familiar with the Supplement because their relatively low ranks excluded them from the loop in which the Supplement had been distributed. The existence of the Supplement, Dostler said, could be proven by interrogating other German generals who were in POW stockades.

From Dostler's point of view, the most egregious issue was the absence at his trial of key witnesses, who could not be located and thus could not testify on his behalf, and the Supplement showing Hitler's order stating, "Under no circumstances can it be permitted, therefore, that a dynamite, sabotage, or terrorist unit simply allows itself to be captured, expecting to be treated according to the rules of the Geneva Convention. The unit must under all circumstances be ruthlessly exterminated."

The Hitler Commando Order, words from Dostler's Supreme Commander, had driven home his duty to obey and execute the OGs.

The court was not listening. Nor did letters requesting clemency and a plea from Dostler's wife and daughter and one from the Vatican have any effect.

Lt. Gen. Matthew Ridgeway, commanding general of the Mediterranean Theater, ordered that Dostler's sentence be carried out at Aversa, Italy, at Peninsular Base Section Stockade No. 1. There, on December 1, he was escorted to the stockade's firing range. Present was a multitude of still and motion picture cameras to record the event. Two enlisted men tied Dostler to a stake. While he was being secured, he asked one of the men to reach into his tunic pocket. In it was a letter to his daughter. A doctor placed a circular piece of white paper over his heart for the executioners to target. A picture shows him tied to the stake looking into a camera. He is surrounded by the enlisted men who secured him to the stake; two chaplains, a German and an American; and a medical doctor.

Anton Dostler was the first and last general and the last German officer to be executed by the Allies in his uniform, wearing his general's epaulets and his officer's cap. The sovereign eagle with the swastika on his uniform and his cap device had been removed.

Dostler was executed at 0909 hours by a firing squad of twelve enlisted men from the 803rd Military Police battalion. At 0911 a military doctor pronounced Dostler dead. He is buried at the Deutscher Soldatenfried-hof cemetery at Pomezi, south of Rome. There, he lies among twenty-seven thousand World War II German dead.

CHAPTER 10

Kesselring Lies

Two seemingly unrelated events included in this narrative—Operation Ginny and the Via Rasella Attack/Ardeatine Cave Massacre—are nevertheless linked to Field Marshal Albert Kesselring, who had a profound impact on the lives of hundreds of people. It is oddly coincidental that the three events took place during the same period—March 23–27, 1944 (Operation Ginny), and March 23–24, 1944 (the Via Rasella Attack and the Ardeatine Cave Massacre).

It should be noted that the Via Rasella Attack and Ardeatine Massacre, which occurred the day after Rasella, are viewed as one event. The Ardeatine Cave Massacre was a reprisal for Italian Partisans' bombing of a column of German police on the Via Rasella in Rome.

Kesselring's involvement in both historical events is complex. But there is linkage between "Smilin' Al" and the murder of the fifteen Ginny OGs and the other two events, although it takes a microscopic perspective and patience to peel away the layers and view the harsh details. Kesselring has often been alternately cheered, derided, ridiculed, and praised throughout the story.

The question is, what is the truth? And how deeply involved were the perjurious Kesselring and his staff?

He surprises, eludes, then wanders off, leaving a haze of questions as he departs the scene for more pressing backstage matters. Every time the curtain falls on him, here he is again, causing us to be suspicious of his character—about why he exited as he did the last time we saw him. What could have been more pressing for him than passing judgment on the lives of not one but fifteen soldiers who had caused no damage while they were free, had caused no injury to either German soldiers or Fascists. In fact, in a brief gunfight before their capture, Lt. Vincent Russo had been wounded in the face by a hand grenade thrown by one of the Germans. The fight lasted about a minute, and that was the end of their freedom until they were executed.

Just when we think we have irrefutable proof of Kesselring's involvement in the Operation Ginny executions, he leaves the stage and surprises us again and again with his subzero smile and his indisputable participation in the deaths of the fifteen OGs on March 26. At every turn, through every interrogation and within anything the field marshal said or put to paper post–World War II, Kesselring denied, simply did not include (or "could not recall"), or obfuscated any part he might have had in approving the execution of the OGs. But he would have us believe that he was an honorable man and honorable men do not lie—particularly a *Generalfeldmarschall*. Kesselring, perhaps, had more influence, more power, than any other officer in deciding the fate of the Ginny OGs. He could have at least temporarily halted the execution process or justified slowing it down, could have said, "Let's review this more closely." His absolute power granted him this option more than anyone else in the Third Reich—except Adolf Hitler.

But like all humans facing a similar situation, Kesselring's first thought had to be "How will this affect me?" "How will history judge me?" Obviously, we know the answer. His first order of business was to obey the *Führerbefehl* and the oaths he took, like all the other soldiers in the Third Reich. Second, it was his business, perhaps more than the others, to take care of himself.

Kesselring's and his staff's actions often refute the polished image of one of the highest-ranking, most-respected general officers in the Wehrmacht. Leading up to his war crimes trials in Venice and Nuremberg, Kesselring and his staff committed multiple cover-ups—not the least of which was destroying all war-related documents—in an attempt to save their popular field marshal, and themselves, from a walk to the gallows. Yet he retained his outstanding reputation and the admiration of both Germans and Allies—not only among his *Waffenbrüder* but also in popular culture.

Because of his stature, military prowess, and grasp of military tactics, he was richly rewarded by Hitler. Financially, the rank of general field marshal was extremely rewarding, and Albert Kesselring was one of the wealthiest generals in the Wehrmacht. In addition to a yearly salary, in 1940 Hitler introduced a tax-free benefit for generals in the range of 2,000 to 4,000 Reichsmarks per month, or $5,000 to $10,000 in US dollars. Hitler also bestowed generous presents on his highest officers, perhaps to buy their loyalty. Kesselring was one of Hitler's favorite officers and admired the way he treated his airmen. For example, Kesselring knew he would never be a match in the air for his professional airmen. Nevertheless, he took his job seriously and learned how to fly, believing it would help him know their jobs.

Albert Kesselring was promoted to general field marshal in 1942 and appointed Commander in Chief South, with overall responsibility for all German operations in the Mediterranean region. He was one of only twenty-four recipients of the Knight's Cross with Oak Leaves, Swords and Diamonds, one of Germany's highest awards. Like other generals of Nazi Germany, he received personal monthly payments from Adolf Hitler—in Kesselring's case 6,000 Reichsmarks ($30,000) per month, a considerable sum. Although these stipends were intended to provide Hitler with undying loyalty from their recipients, they did not always work as Hitler had intended.

And while Kesselring was a Hitler favorite, he actually was promoted to commander of Air Fleet II (*Luftflotte II*) as a result of another general's misfortune—by sheer luck, one might say—which involved the Mechelen Affair on January 10, 1940.

Erich Hoenmanns was flying a Messerschmitt Bf 108 *Taifun* (Typhoon), a reconnaissance two-seater. In the back seat of the small aircraft, Major Helmuth Reinberger was carrying strategic plans for operation *Fall Gelb* (Case Yellow), the German attack on the Lowlands. However, the little Typhoon crash-landed near Vucht, Belgium, because Hoenmanns—nervous about carrying such top-secret plans—mistook the fuel supply lever for the throttle. (Today, there is a discreet monument in a pastoral field where the Typhoon crashed.) The incident produced an immediate crisis, although one that abated relatively quickly. However, this security breach enraged Hitler and humiliated *Reichsmarschall* (Marshal of the Reich) Hermann Göring. To save face, Göring, without hesitation, fired *Luftflotte II's* commanding officer, the "Old Eagle," Hellmuth Felmy, and replaced him with Kesselring. Announcing the appointment, Göring did not keep his cards close to his vest, saying, "Kesselring got the job because I have nobody else." So Kesselring was in the right place at the right time.

There have been numerous accounts of Kesselring's involvement in the Ginny massacre. But his popularity among his men, his deep loyalty to Hitler, and his general popularity among both Germans and Allies have done much to hide Kesselring's crimes.

The scope of Kesselring's involvement in the Ginny executions is irrefutable. Still, his popularity among his *truppen* (troops) and numerous Allies after the war had much to do with the commutation of his death sentence for war crimes—and not only for the deaths of the American commandos.

It was impossible for Kesselring to avoid mentioning his trial in his book, and he skillfully hedged about where he was on March 23–24, 1944. He leaves us, unsuspecting readers, believing he was nowhere other than the Cassino front and Monte Soratte. However, in a sworn statement in London on September 26, 1945, he said the following:

"At the time of the outrage, I was not at my battle HQ, being extremely occupied by the events on the Gagliano [Cassino front]. At my battle HQ in the last hours of the 23rd March [Westphal reported to me the incident in Via Rasella.]"

All this subterfuge regarding Kesselring's particulars cannot hide some of the lesser-known illegalities he is associated with—although most diminished under the glow of his reputation. For example:

In late March 1945, high-level German officers—Colonel Vietinghoff, Lieutenant General Röttiger, and others—were involved in bizarre, complicated negotiations to end the Wehrmacht's war effort in Italy, which had long been hopeless. For their involvement, Kesselring ordered their arrests and executions. They probably would have been shot if Hitler's suicide on April 30 had not interfered with Kesselring's plans.

Kesselring also ordered the summary execution of German officers in Munich who had attempted to take control and surrender the city to the approaching US Army.

There is no question that Kesselring won over many admirers at his trials. The day he was sentenced, May 7, 1947, a British major told Kesselring, "Field Marshal, you have no idea how much you have won the respect of all British officers during your trial, and especially today." Kesselring, audacious after week after week of rendering lie after lie to the court, replied, "Major, if I had behaved one iota differently, I would never have deserved to become a German field marshal."

Dr. Hans Laternser, Kesselring's attorney, observed that everyone in the courtroom was moved and felt that Kesselring had won his last victory. A British guard told Laternser, "Give the Field Marshal the regards of a British private. Tell him that all my thoughts are with him and that I hope he will be acquitted.... For he is a fine soldier." No one among those who had high praise for the field marshal had the slightest notion of who the real "Smilin' Al" was. He had successfully duped so many.

Even Kesselring's attorney was drawn into his cloud of lies. In his closing remarks to the court, Laternser had high praises for his client, saying:

> Anyone who has seen the Field Marshal during the two weeks of his being questioned will have gained the conviction that this man has never attempted to speak an untruth. His sometimes-complicated answers could always be traced back to [his] desire to discover the truth himself, to serve the truth, and to let the truth be victorious even it if were at as his own expense. Can any man who has seen the Field Marshal as a soldier believe that he has not the courage to stand by the truth? One who has carried out fairly the battle against the enemy in this most difficult battle of his life by a lack of truth. This is my conviction, that full credence must be as to the sworn statement of the Field Marshal himself.

Not until half a century later did the truth finally emerge. *Oberst* (Colonel) Dietrich Beelitz, Kesselring's intelligence officer and fellow conspirator, admitted that the documents shown to him in 1997 were accurate: Kesselring had been in Liguria, not Monte Soratte, on March 24, 1944. Kesselring had been lying all the time.

CHAPTER 11

Via Rasella

A HALF MILE FROM THE TREVI FOUNTAIN IN ROME IS VIA RASELLA, A narrow, sloped street named for a property owned by the Rasella family. At 1545 hours on March 24, 1944, it would become the site of the Via Rasella Attack (*Attaco di Via Rasella*), another immeasurably grotesque page in WWII history. Linked to the execution of 335 partisans, it would be one of the largest massacres of the war.

Every day a company of 142 uniformed German *Ordnungspolizei* (Order Police, or ORPO) would conclude rifle practice at a nearby firing range around 1500 hours and march eastward on the Via Rasella toward their quarters in Marco Barracks in the Castro Pretorius complex, northwest of Rome's main railroad terminal.

On either side of the narrow cobblestone streets were antiquated four-story walk-up apartment buildings. Two shops and a café are spread out on the street level. Although a significant action against the German occupiers had been contemplated since the German occupation of Rome, none of the proposed ideas or actions seemed effective enough to carry out. Carlo Bentivegna, code name Polo, was a medical doctor and Italian partisan who had been calling for a significant uprising by his fellow citizens: "The SS, who daily march through the Via Rasella at the same hours, must be killed."

During WWII, while studying medicine at university, Bentivegna joined the Italian Communist Party. He became an active member of the guerrilla groups organized by the Roman resistance following the occupation of Italy by Nazi Germany. Although Bentivegna and fellow partisan twenty-five-year-old Mario Fiorentini were members of the Patriotic Action Group (*Gruppi di Azione Patriottica*, or GAP), none of their plans seemed capable of dealing a deadly blow to the Germans without costing their own lives in the process—until Fiorentini recognized an opportunity right under his nose.

Fiorentini lived in Apartment 18 Via Capo le Case with his wife. Looking north from his apartment, he became aware of a recurring event he had never paid mind to before: a column of German policemen marching under his window and going up Via Rasella toward their quarters at Marco Barracks. He let it go for a few days but occasionally checked out the window at the same time—3:00 p.m.

Fiorentini devised a plan to attack the marching Germans and presented it to his confederates. They said it was too simple. Florentino went back to his pad and pencil—and his stopwatch. A few days later, another idea struck, one that coincided with a significant date in Italian history: March 23, 1919, the date Benito Mussolini had founded the Fascist Party of Italy in Milan. Fiorentini's idea was to build an attack around that date. Now, in 1944, the new Fascists (*Partito Fascista Repubblicano*, or PFR) in Rome were planning a celebration, a commemoration to mark the historic date established by Il Duce in 1919. Fiorentini and his partisan comrades figured this would be an auspicious time to encourage the citizens of Rome, who were insufficiently united and lacked the strength in both numbers and spirit, to take action against their German oppressors.

A couple of days went by, and there were no marching German policemen on Via Rasella. But this was good: It gave Fiorentini more time to polish his new plan, which this time would involve a large bomb. He discarded his previous plan, to drop dozens of hand grenades from the windows and roofs of the buildings on Via Rasella, and designed another—simply go down onto Via Rasella, machine-gun the unsuspecting ORPO, and then flee the area. But, brave as he was, Fiorentini was not in a sacrificial mood; neither were his men. It had to be a remote attack.

The final plan evolved, and just in time, because the German policemen were back on their old schedule, marching robustly up the narrow Via Rasella every day at the same time, 1500–1530 hours.

First, Fiorentini recruited more than a dozen GAP comrades to participate in the attack; it would be, they all agreed, the most extensive operation in Rome the partisans had ever undertaken. The Germans in Rome had been attacked before, but this one would be the biggest, the most bold.

The primary weapon would be a powerful single bomb—"*La bomba*," they called it. Packed into a cylindrical steel case, the bomb contained twelve kilograms of trinitrotoluene (TNT), or 4.44 pounds of lethal explosive, and an assortment of nuts and bolts—enough to create a gigantic kill zone, cause much damage to the surrounding area and surely kill many of the policemen in the column. They divided six additional kilograms of TNT among smaller pieces of iron tubing. The iron pipes were a deliberate selection to pack the bomb. After ignition, the pipe would splinter and send out a deluge of nuts and bolts and steel shrapnel, further increasing the bomb's kill capacity. The most challenging part of implementing the plan was timing the marchers from the moment they started on Via Rasella until they reached the end of the street. The large bomb was certainly not a twenty-first-century piece of precision technology triggered by cellular phone or radio signals. It was set off by an old-fashioned fuse, the kind found in Fourth of July firecrackers. The length of the fuse and material determined the time it took to burn into the TNT and set it off. The partisans crafted a fuse that would burn for forty seconds and tested the timing until they were certain it would set off the TNT at the appropriate time. Timing and stealth were at the heart of their plan.

On this day, *La bomba* would be used to kill as many German police as possible.

It took the GAP a day or two to acquire the TNT, obtain the fuses and time them, and obtain the pipes that would hold the TNT. Then they focused on the logistics of igniting *La bomba* at just the right second—timing how long it took the marchers from the start of Via Rasella to the point of detonation. They went about their work with unbound enthusiasm, this time believing their plan would substantially motivate the population to revolt against the Germans. It did not.

The thought of possible reprisals did not deter their efforts. They had to have known that after the attack, the Germans would be after them and punish them—as well as innocent people—with unbound vengeance.

But to the partisans, it was the only alternative: They either passively accepted the Germans' occupation of their homeland or made sacrifices of their own lives and the lives of others.

Although the GAP members wished to kill all the ORPO marching on Via Rasella, they knew *La bomba*, as big as it was, would not kill all 142 marchers. The partisans would be satisfied if they took down 50 percent of the marching police. They estimated that the explosion would kill innocent pedestrians as well—which did not deter them. They were hell-bent on killing as many German policemen as possible. The attack would show the Germans how much they were hated, and that killing civilians was worth the sacrifice. More than anything, they wanted the attack to show how motivated they were, how intent they were on getting rid of the German presence. Sadly, their experience didn't match their bravery.

On Via Rasella waited Carla Capponi, Raul Falcioni, Fernando Vitagliano, Pasquale Balsamo, Francesco Curreli, Guglielmo Blasi, Mario Fiorentini, and Marisa Musu, who provided cover fire by using a mortar. Three of the partisans, using grenade-like bombs and a pistol, would attack the column before it reached the Via Quattro Fontane. Two GAP members were assigned to time the marchers from the beginning of Via Rasella to the abandoned Palazzo Tittoni at No. 156 Via Rasella, the predetermined spot where *La bomba* would be set off; it would take 140 seconds for the marchers to cover 250-meter-long Via Rasella. They further calculated that the entire column would be on Via Rasella for approximately ninety seconds, their rifles on their shoulders, showing their pride to the citizens.

The bomb was hidden in a large canvas bag, placed in a cart, and pushed by Carlo Bentivegna, disguised as a street cleaner, who would ignite the fuse; with him was a lookout, another member of the GAP.

A partisan down the street would signal them once he saw the marchers' column approaching the start of Via Rasella. He would signal again when the first policemen at the head of the column came to within forty seconds of the garbage cart—still another fifteen seconds short of the Via Quattro Fontane, the spot where *La bomba* was intended to go off. Once the bomb was ignited, the GAP force would scatter and blend into the city populace.

And so, here comes the marching column approaching Via Rasella . . .

At that moment, the *Bozen* column consisted of 142 German soldiers wearing dark gray steel helmets with their distinctive green, white, and gold *Ordnungspolizei* decals on the temporal sides. They were wearing their field uniforms with the ORPO insignia and carrying the rifles they had just used to practice at the firing range. Proud of who they were, they marched with military precision—almost arrogantly—ever tense, however, and mindful of a possible attack from partisans. The latter wanted to see all of them either dead or out of Rome. This magnificent, historic city had been a place of relaxation for the Germans, but at this stage in the war, it was no longer so. Now, every day, Rome was a danger zone.

And so noted Field Marshal Kesselring: "Rome became for us an explosive city. [. . .] For us, the security of the rear guard of the frontline was a severe issue. The morale of our troops [was] directly affected since they could not be safely sent to Rome anymore for short periods of rest."

An assignment to Rome could prove just as lethal as serving in battle. German soldiers who had once looked forward to R & R in Rome no longer wished to go there. On the battlefield you at least knew who the enemy was because they were wearing uniforms—the partisans, however, were not distinguishable from the rest of the populace. The fear of attacks by the partisans at any time and by any means was very real. No longer could the German occupiers casually stroll around the city and feel safe in cafes, restaurants, and movie theaters. The Italians had had enough of the Germans, and ambushes such as the one on Via Rasella were not out of the question.

The Germans here were under the command of the German Command of the City of Rome, which was headed by Luftwaffe *Generalleutnant* (Lieutenant General) Kurt Mälzer, who would be convicted of war crimes at the war's end. Mälzer, puffy, malicious, and vindictive, had complete control of the Wehrmacht troops' garrison and, nominally, the SS troops throughout the city.

It was now approaching 1545 hours, and one of the German policemen locked eyes with the first partisan lookout. Whether the policeman knew what was about to happen did not matter, because he would be dead within the next second. There were other lookouts at strategic points; one, Marisa Masu, would also launch 45mm mortar shells.

The company of German police marched eastward on Via Rasella toward their quarters at the Marco Barracks, unaware of the impending attack. Most were of Italian extraction and had served in Russia in the Italian army. Initially designated Police Regiment South Tyrol, the company was raised in 1943 from older residents of Bolzano. Soon, because of their age—they averaged thirty-five years—it became apparent that they were unsuitable for military service at the brutal Eastern Front. They were then formed into the 11th Company, 3rd Battalion, German Police Regiment Bolzano (*Bozen*). Their uniform color was a dark grass green—thus their nickname: "Green Police" (*Grüne Polizei*). With their emblem worn on their uniforms and metal devices on their caps, there was no mistaking them for the SS.

In a photograph taken minutes after the explosion, a crowd of fifteen civilians, some with their hands locked behind their heads, are standing at the front gate at the Galleria Nazionale d'Arte Antica, which houses the main national collection of older paintings in Rome. They are facing armed Order Police with their distinctive white, green, and gold police insignia; at that moment, there are no signs of the SS.

The marchers were now seconds away from Via Quattro Fontane. The fuse on *La bomba* had already been lit by Bentivegna, who then escaped along with the other sixteen GAF perpetrators.

When *La bomba* was detonated, the explosion was so loud that it was heard throughout the city of Rome—a ringing, battering basso of thunder and hellfire. Via Rasella vanished in a cloak of black smoke, a stone and cement carapace over the dead and dying. In the immediate zone of the blast were bloody, mutilated bodies, a tangle of indistinguishable body parts. Some victims were trying to crawl away but getting nowhere because they were sightless. Others held up arms without hands. Others pleaded for help—without hearing their own agony. Shoes, clothing, and shreds of brightly colored cloth, marred by the brilliance and peculiar patterns of blood, redder than red, lay among the dead and dying. The cobblestones were covered in blood and body parts. Wooden door and window frames hung askew; walls of the buildings lining the street were pocked and gouged by shrapnel from the steel casings that had contained the TNT's fury.

In less than a minute, the air screamed with ululating sirens from police vans and ambulances. The entire world seemed to be dying here on this one street cradled in the ancient city of Rome, a city that had never seen such bloodshed as this moment at 1545 hours, which would come to be known as *Attacco di Via Rasella*—the Via Rasella Attack.

It was estimated that the *Bozen* marchers sustained 60 percent casualties in less than two seconds. According to a witness at the Kesselring trial, thirty-two *polizei* were killed instantly, another four to six were expected to die, and eleven were wounded. At least two Italian civilians, bystanders, were killed, but little was said about their deaths.

The GAF achieved no measurable results from their efforts except the dead and the dying: The police killed were not SS troops. The major insurrection Italians pined for—an unprecedented uprising—did not ensue. The population did not stand up to the Germans any more than they had before. Instead—and all Italians knew this—a reprisal of unprecedented madness would descend upon them.

The Germans were beyond infuriated. That their troops here in this supposed oasis of quiet and rest had taken such a profound hit was incomprehensible and stirred up the most vicious venom their souls possessed.

The Germans, fearful that this attack was the beginning of an Allied breakout from the Anzio/Netruno beachhead that would roll into a headlong attack against them, strengthened their security in every aspect of an already suffering Roman population.

SS-Obersturmbannführer (Lieutenant Colonel) Herbert Kappler was eating lunch at the Excelsior Hotel on the Via Veneto and lurched from his table upon hearing the explosion. He arrived at the frenetic scene two minutes later to supervise the investigation, which was already under way. He was Gestapo chief of Rome and the *Oberbefehlshaber des Sicherheitspolizei und SS* (Chief of SiPo) and SS Police Chief of the City's *Ordnungspolizei*. In early 1944 Kappler was the highest representative of the Reich Security Main Office in Rome. He answered directly to both the military governorship under Luftwaffe General Kurt Mälzer (another war criminal), as well as the SS chain of command under the Higher SS and Police Leader of Italy, SS-*Obergruppenführer* (Lieutenant General) Karl Wolff. Wolff, whom we have met earlier, was the friend and former classmate who saved the life of Wilhelm Hermann Alexander Fürst zu Dohna-Schlobitten, discharged with his life from the Wehrmacht for refusing to order the execution of the Ginny OGs. In his official capacity, Kappler often came into direct conflict with the Vatican, having a strong suspicion that Pope Pius XII was harboring Jews and Allied fugitives and escaped prisoners, even though the Vatican was technically neutral. Kappler's main adversary in this respect was Monsignor Hugh O'Flaherty, whose activities helping Jewish fugitives and Allied prisoners escape from Rome led to Kappler marking him for assassination. (Paradoxically, after the war, Kappler and O'Flaherty became friends.) Kappler served in both the German police and security service—the *Sicherheitspolizei* and the SD—in the city of Rome. In this regard, Kappler's SD included the *Geheime Staatspolizei*, aka the Gestapo. (**Note:** Kappler was imprisoned in Italy by the Americans but escaped from prison; he died in West Germany in 1978.) After the Germans occupied Rome, Kappler was appointed *Ober-befehlsaber des Sicherheitspolizei und SD* (Chief of the Security Police and Security Service) for all SS and Order Police throughout the city.

Before the blast subsided, Luftwaffe General Kurt Mälzer, who was drinking his lunch and thus inebriated, arrived on the scene agitated and in a rage. He soon began trying to order his men to acquire large amounts of TNT. Screaming and cursing, waving his pistol, he threatened to use the explosives to destroy every house on Via Rasella. He then ordered his police to acquire many liters of gasoline, enough to burn everything in the center of Rome to cinders. After a few minutes, Kappler intervened, calmed Mälzer down, and convinced him to leave the scene and leave the investigation up to him. Meanwhile, the Order Police, with weapons drawn, had rounded up dozens of Italians, ordering them to lock their hands behind their heads. The roundup and questioning continued, but none of the partisans were caught.

Again, at Kesselring's trial, Kappler testified that none of the Italian partisans had been captured at Via Rasella. Several weeks after the attack, two were caught by the Italian Fascist police but later escaped.

Since Rome had become a city close to the fighting front, Mälzer had been given the authority to invoke retaliatory measures against all partisans following approval of the senior commanders of the Wehrmacht:

Generaloberst (Colonel General) Eberhard von Mackensen, commander of AOK 14 (Fourteenth Army), and Albert Kesselring. In this respect, *SS-Obersturmbannführer* Herbert Kappler, the Gestapo chief, was Mälzer's subordinate.

A couple of hours after the attack, at around 1700 hours, Kappler and Mälzer knew the work ahead would be most severe and highly deadly. They had to organize the planning, ratios, and logistics of the reprisal that certainly would have to be taken immediately. They agreed that a 10:1 execution ratio was suitable—ten partisans would be executed for one killed policeman. However, they also knew that a higher authority—Hitler, certainly—would soon intervene with his own suggestions, and they were not going to be as lenient as theirs. Nevertheless, they were required to examine the situation and offer their recommendations; it was complex.

For the sake of expediency and clarity, the following is the chain of events that led to the murder of more than three hundred Italian citizens the next day in reprisal for the attack on Via Rasella:

- *Oberst* (Colonel) Dietrich Beelitz, Kesselring's chief of operations (at thirty-eight, the youngest general in the Wehrmacht), cautions Luftwaffe General Kurt Mälzer against "burning and razing" all the houses on Via Rasella and eradicating the center of Rome through the use of dynamite and gasoline. He condemns a "knee-jerk reaction."
- Beelitz reports the "outrage" to *Generalmajor* (Major General) Horst Freiherr Treusch von Buttlar-Brandenfels—commonly referred to as Treusch—of the OKW's Army Operations Staff, located in the northwestern suburbs of Rome; he relates details of the attack. Beelitz speaks with both Mackensen and *Oberst* (Colonel) Wolfgang Hauser, Mackensen's chief of staff.
- Between 1600 and 1700, Beelitz attempts to contact Westphal, Kesselring's chief of staff. He leaves word that Westphal should return immediately to Kesselring's HQ in Monte Soratte and advise Kesselring of the earlier attack at Via Rasella.
- Von Buttlar-Brandenfels tells Beelitz that the Führer has already been apprised and that he is in a state of "rage." He is contemplating kill ratios and will get back to them.

- Beelitz tells OKW that he believes Kesselring will oppose a 100:1 kill ratio—this number is stunning.
- Between 1600 and 1700, von Buttlar-Brandenfels and another officer telephone Beelitz. Hitler, Treusch tells Beelitz, is in a "dog attack frenzy" that is growing by the minute. While Hitler previously wanted a 50:1 kill ratio, he now wants a 100:1 ratio. Further, AOK 14 is ordered to investigate the matter and recommend a course of action they believe is reasonable as soon as possible. Beelitz asks von Buttlar-Brandenfels if he would attempt to get Hitler to amend his 100:1 ratio.
- Between 1730 and 1800 hours, Mälzer calls Mackensen at AOK 14. Mälzer has spoken to Gestapo Chief Kappler about the reprisals. He orders Kappler to his office to discuss the matter.
- Kappler, now at Mälzer's office, agrees that the execution of ten Italians for one dead policeman is appropriate. From his office, Mälzer and Kappler speak via telephone to Mackensen and inform him that the 10:1 execution ratio seems reasonable. Mackensen agrees.
- Again, Westphal requests von Buttlar-Brandenfels to try to soften Hitler's 100:1 ratio, which would amount to rounding up and executing more than three thousand (probably) innocent Italians and lead to a massive Italian revolt and condemnation by the world. They both agree that Hitler's number is absurd.
- Westphal endorses the 10:1 ratio. Mackensen, Kappler, and Mälzer report this to Hauser, who sends the agreement to OKW/Hitler at Berchtesgaden, Hitler's home/headquarters.
- Hauser reports to Westphal that "14 Army had come to an agreement with Kappler, and according to [it] only people should be taken [for the reprisal] who had already been condemned to death." (Kappler knew this would be impossible because he did not have near that many condemned to death in his prisons.)
- Kappler tells Mackensen and Mälzer that in earlier cases of such reprisals, he was able to find enough "suitable candidates" for execution from "death-worthy" candidates.
- The 10:1 ratio everyone had agreed on was not sent to Hitler because Monte Soratte (Kesselring) knew that Hitler would insist on the execution of "innocents" and would reject victims on whom death sentences already had been imposed.

- From Berchtesgaden, von Buttlar-Brandenfels passed on a *Führer befehl* from Hitler; it says: "The Führer [has]issued an order that for every German police officer killed [in the Via Rasella] ten Italian hostages should be shot." It says nothing about innocents versus criminals already sentenced to death.
- Kesselring, listening in on the call, after hanging up said, "And I can tell you [Beelitz, Westphal, and Buttlar-Brandenfels] that I just hung up with Kappler and he told me he had a sufficiently big number of people who had been sentenced to death for this reprisal action. . . . I thanked him, and that was the end of the conversation."
- Kesselring, Westphal, and Beelitz all said they felt relieved, because now only criminals, not innocents as Hitler demanded, would be executed.
- Later, at his trial, Kesselring swore that "this information for me— the *Führerbefehl*—from Hitler's headquarters, constituted for me an order. And there was no other alternative."
- Kesselring then instructed Westphal to transmit the *Führerbefehl* down to AOK 14.
- But then, the matter—kill ratios, innocent people versus criminals, and so on—would turn once again, as is evident here through Kesselring's chief of staff, General Westphal, as a witness at Kesselring's trial:

Judge Advocate:	The first time that you came into the picture was after 1700 hours on the 23rd; is that right?
Westphal:	Yes.
Judge Advocate:	And when did you first realize there had been what was called an agreement or an arrangement between Kappler and General Mackensen?
Westphal:	Shortly before the Field Marshal arrived.
Judge Advocate:	Let us see. At about 5 o'clock on the afternoon of the 23rd, did you understand that an arrangement had been made whereby no innocent person would be killed in this reprisal?
Westphal:	I did not.

Judge Advocate:	When you got Hitler's order, did you understand from that order that you were to pick people who really mattered for the community and shoot them as an example?
Westphal:	Which order?
Judge Advocate:	[The first Hitler/OKW order—the *Führerbefehl*]; Hitler Order No. 2 will be described below].
Westphal:	That was Hitler's intention, that that should happen.
Judge Advocate:	Have you any doubt, General Westphal, that that is what he meant?
Westphal:	No, it is quite certain that that was his intention what you just said, and not that convicted people should be shot.
Judge Advocate:	You know perfectly well, General Westphal, that Hitler would have been in the most violent rage, would he not, if he had heard the suggestion was to shoot, by way of reprisal, perhaps a criminal already sentenced to death?
Westphal:	That was one of our great worries and we talked about it. Beelitz and myself, in the evening.
Judge Advocate:	Is it clear that when you got the order [the *Führerbefehl*], as you say, from General [Treusch von Buttlar] to carry out a reprisal in a ratio of 10 to 1, that the Field Marshal [Kesselring], at about half past eight on the night of [March 23], considered it and agreed that it should be carried out and gave you an order to pass it on?
Westphal:	Yes, but in the form that not innocent people should be taken for the reprisal, but in the way as it had been agreed to between [Kesselring] and [Kappler].
Judge Advocate:	It is quite clear that at or about half past eight on the night of the 23rd the Field Marshal had accepted responsibility for carrying out the reprisal of the Wehrmacht?

Westphal: Yes, but that is a very essential point that I want to emphasize, only under the condition that Kappler's [prisoners] who had been sentenced to death, would be taken for this reprisal.

. . . . .

Judge Advocate: General Westphal, at 8:30 you, Beelitz, and the Field Marshal had entered into what I call a conspiracy to shoot people who you say you knew were already sentenced to death for some crime and which you knew would never have satisfied Hitler[,] and he would have stopped it the moment he heard of it?

Westphal: Yes.

Judge Advocate: Were you and Beelitz and the Field Marshal then prepared to risk your careers?

Westphal: Yes, Beelitz and myself are only responsible to the Field Marshal and obey his orders. The Field Marshal is responsible to Hitler.

. . . . .

Judge Advocate: I am afraid you will be in the witness box all day, because I know what I am putting to you and I want to keep to that point. You passed on an order to the 14th Army which was [a] deliberate[,] calculated breach of Hiller's order?

Westphal: Yes.

Judge Advocate: Is it right that when a Field Marshal gets a military order from a person who he has taken his oath to obey loyally that he is entitled to disobey that order?

Westphal: I think that only a human being who has been confronted with the situation with which we were confronted for years can judge this question.

Judge Advocate: I am not criticizing. Is not the position, quite clearly, that the Field Marshal was deliberately and knowingly disobeying the oath that he had taken to Hitler?

Westphal:	Looked at from one point of view that might be so, but from a soldier's point of view that was not so.
Judge Advocate:	You are a high[-]ranking Wehrmacht officer. Did it never occur to you to say to the Field Marshal: "Sir, you are a Field Marshal; do not let us be a party to some agreement of this kind with an SD lieutenant colonel. Let us do the right thing. Let us get on right now to Keitel and Jodl and put our views forcibly before Hitler[,] and if Hitler will insist on this barbarous order then he can do something about it." Did it never occur to you that the Field Marshal was putting himself in a very ignominious position?
Westphal:	For five years we were trying to get our view put across to the people at the top[;] for five years we had no success. It would have been senseless to have done it.
Judge Advocate:	Do you think it is senseless? It is better to lose our self-respect; is that what you feel? To the senior officer, it is better to lose his self-respect than to say simply to Hitler: "I cannot carry out this order. You can do what you like about it?"
Westphal:	I do not know what anyone should lose one's self-respect if one tries very hard not to kill innocent people but to kill the guilty ones.

Dr. Laternser then asked Westphal: "What happened after [you received] this Jodl order" [the second *Führerbefehl*]?

Westphal:	First of all I looked at my notes with regard to this order and thought quietly about [it], and I thought also about the rather unfriendly telephone conversation which we had, Jodl and myself[;] then I spoke with Beelitz[,] and after this conversation, we were convinced, both of us, that we had nothing to do anymore with this matter. I asked Beelitz to come

	into my office because I wanted to talk to him about it and, as far as I remember, parts of the conversation [had been] listened into by Beelitz.
Dr. Laternser:	When did you inform Kesselring of the second *Führerbefehl*?
Westphal:	I awakened him in his room and he answered the phone.
Dr. Laternser:	[To the witness] No, General, you were speaking about your report of the new order to the Field Marshal. Now, what did the Field Marshal say to you when you informed him of the order given you by Jodl [the second *Führerbefehl*]?
Westphal:	"I agree[:] pass on the order [to AOK 14].

CHAPTER 12

Reprisals

On the afternoon of March 23, Kappler, Mackensen, Hauser, and Mälzer agreed that a ten-for-one execution would be appropriate. Kappler, now sure there would be an execution, set off on selecting and naming the victims. Currently, there were twenty-eight dead police officers. After checking his "inventory," Kappler soon realized that he would not be able find 280 "death-worthy" Italians in his SS jails.

Sometime that evening, March 23, at around 2100 hours, he telephoned *SS-Brigadeführer und Generalmajor der Polizei* Dr. Wilhelm Harster, Kappler's immediate superior, in Verona; they went over the situation for about twenty minutes. They concluded that "fifty-seven Jews who were in Kappler's prisons as a result of a general order must be added to the list if necessary to make up the balance." Before he hung up, Harster added, "If there is no other possibility at all, well then you cannot help taking those too." By 2300 hours that night, Kappler continued to hastily pore through his lists. He was able to find 4 inmates who had been condemned to death by a legitimate court, 17 serving long terms of imprisonment, 167 who were "death-worthy," and about 17 others serving long terms of imprisonment whose sentences were "pending." "Additionally, about two to four had been rounded up as suspects around Via Rasella immediately after the attack and were implicated in the attack." Some potential victims were pulled out of their apartments on no evidence of involvement whatsoever.

By noon the next day, Kappler felt he had made progress and met with Mälzer, showing him the nominal roll containing the names of 269 to 271 victims he had gleaned from his files. At this time, thirty-two police officers had died; the thirty-third would soon follow.

Kappler had to make up the deficit somehow. He called the Italian chief of police in Rome, with whom he had a good relationship and who had previously promised Kappler that he would help find Italians from his own jails, "using the same measuring stick that Kappler had been using." Mälzer got Kappler's assurance that things were going to work out. Every name on Kappler's list had a notation with the type of crime they had committed. In the *Führerbefehl* issued the previous evening, Hitler had decreed the executions must be completed and reported within twenty-four hours.

Now Mälzer and Kappler discussed the logistics of the heinous crime that was about to be committed. They decided that each victim had to be shot from behind at close range at the base of the skull and by a single executioner using a single bullet.

During this repugnant conversation, *Major der Polizei* (Police Major) Hellmuth Dobrick from the 3rd Battalion, Police Regiment Bolzano, to which the 11th had previously belonged, was present. At first, he agreed that this form of execution would be appropriate for his men to be part of the firing squad. However, when he learned how the shooting would be carried out—one shot at the base of the skull—he demurred.

"My men," Bolzano said, "are old. They are partly very religious, partly full of superstition[,] and they came from very far away provinces of the Alps. . . .If these people should be shot [in this fashion at short range] then I cannot ask my men to do [it]." Kappler and Mälzer accepted this excuse, but then Mälzer told Kappler, "Well, then, you have to do it." Kappler, too, wanted no part of the executions himself and asked Mälzer to leave him out of it. Mälzer called Hauser, but the latter ruled: "The police are the victims, and the police will take on the reprisals as well." Mälzer said to Kappler, "You see, there is nothing that can be done. You have got to take care of the matter."

Here now descends another contradiction in the trial testimony of Kappler, who had agreed with Westphal, Beelitz, and Hauser that the ten-for-one reprisal was Hitler's will as he expressed it in the first *Füh rerbefehl*. But Kappler had insisted it was Hauser who, at noon on the 24th, had arbitrarily ordered his Gestapo to assume responsibility for the executions. In essence, he was denying the sworn testimonies of

Kesselring, Westphal, Beelitz, and Zolling that there had been a second *Führerbefehl* passed from Jodl to Westphal to Hauser at AOK 14 and then through the Commandant of Rome to Kappler on the morning of March 24. When Westphal received the *Führerbefehl*, he woke Kesselring and informed him of the order. Kesselring told him to send it down to AOK for implementation.

At trial, this was one of Kesselring's big lies, of which Westphal was also part: Both denied that Kesselring had told Westphal to send the order to AOK 14.

After receiving the order from Hauser to proceed with the executions, Kappler went to his office on Via Tasso. There, in a meeting with his entire staff, he informed his sixty officers and men what they must do: They, including Kappler, had to take part in the actual shootings.

The site chosen was the Fosse Ardeatine caves a little beyond the famous Appian Way, near the catacombs of Saint Calixtus and Saint Domitilla. This was a suitable site, Kappler informed his men, because after the executions, the area would be dynamited and bulldozed, serving as a convenient gravesite; the dead would not have to be trucked anywhere. The caves, formed of sandstone, were very deep, he told them, and went on underground and divided into various corridors. Before the first truckloads of victims arrived, Kappler made a personal inspection.

At the prisons, the victims' arms were tied behind their backs. They then were tied together in groups of five, loaded onto the trucks, and transported to the caves; they were not told of their fate.

The trucks arrived at the caves, and in groups of five, the victims were "escorted" into the caves, it is assumed still unsuspecting, with an SS man behind them. Every other SS man carried a flashlight, which were placed along the walls of the caves' tunnels. Once in the tunnels, the victims were ordered to kneel. On a command issued by one of the SS officers, each victim was shot once (twice if necessary) in the brain stem; German and Italian machine pistols were used. As soon as one group of five had been shot, the next group was brought in. Before moving on, each victim had to be inspected by "the Sanitary Department," a medic of sorts, to be certain of death. In several cases it was necessary to deliver a coup de grâce. And so it went throughout the afternoon and the evening.

The first victim was killed at 1400 hours on March 24. After about 75 percent of the victims had been killed, Kappler went into the cave and inspected the bodies, shooting one of the victims from the second group who was still alive. Assured that everything was running smoothly, Kappler returned to Via Tasso to take a break, returning to the caves around 1800 hours.

"On arrival," he said, "I found that *SS-Hauptsturmführer* Wetje had not fired a shot. I spoke to him in a comradely manner and then went into the cave with him to fire a shot at the same time as he."

At 2030 hours, March 24, the final round was fired by an executioner; all the victims were dead.

By this time, thirty-three policemen had died. Yet seldom does one see any mention of the civilian casualties as a result of *La Bomba*, and there seem to have been more than a few.

Now, another problem: It was soon discovered that 335—not 330—corpses were strewn about the cave's blood-slicked floor. *SS-Hauptsturmführer* Carl Schütz had been the scorekeeper along with *SS-Hauptsturmführer* Erich Priebke (more about him later), both checking off the names of the victims as they alighted from the trucks.

What about those five additional victims?

Kappler later concluded that they had been in the consignment from the Italian jails and were simply the result of a "miscount."

At the trial again, Colonel Halse, the prosecutor, picked up the questioning:

Col. Halse: Now with regard to the [victims supplied by the Italian police[;] you had not received a list [of these at the time of the shooting]?

Kappler: Not yet.

Col. Halse: When did you receive that list?

Kappler: I believe I had seen that nominal roll only on the following day.

Col. Halse: That is the 25th?

Kappler: Yes.

Col. Halse: Do you know how many people from the Italian custody
                were in fact taken to the Ardeatine Caves?

Kappler: I was reported the figure 25.

Col. Halse: How many people were in fact shot on that day by your
                Außennkommando?

Kappler: 335.

Col. Halse: That was more than the 10-to-1 ratio. Can you explain
                that?

Kappler: I had heard only on the next day from [Schütz]—or was
                it Kripe [Priebke], I am not quite certain—that 335 were
                shot. I asked immediately questions and I have investi-
                gated myself. I came to the following conclusion: that the
                Italian nominal roll contained, instead of only 50 names,
                55, but at that time when the people were shot it was not
                checked[,] and it was assumed that only 50 were there. I
                heard about it only on the following day. I heard that ap-
                parently the names were checked by then were not count-
                ed at the same time.

Kappler returned to Via Tasso and reported to Bohm: "Execution carried
out." He did not mention, however, at the time or later, that his *Außenn-
kommando* had shot five more than had been stipulated in the *Führerbefehl*.

Today the name Kappler is probably unknown to most except for
serious military historians. *Hauptsturmführer* Erich Priebke is better
known—he was one of the shooters at the Ardeatine Caves and the
"scorekeeper" of the victims coming off the trucks that day and rose from
obscurity to become a hunted international war criminal wanted by both
Italian and German courts. He had also worked for Kappler between
Kappler's official office and the Holy See. Priebke is a typical example of
"Befehl ist Befehl"—"an order is an order"—a conviction steadfastly maintained throughout the German ranks. Claiming he was obeying orders,
Priebke admitted killing two people in the Ardeatine Caves. He would
later deny this admission.

The Italian police arrested Priebke in the summer of 1945 for his
participation in the Ardeatine Massacre, but he escaped from a British

stockade at Rimini, Italy. He also worked for and received help from ODESSA, the Organization of Former SS Members (*Organisation Der Ehemaligen SS-Angehörigen*), and fled to Argentina, where he lived for more than fifty years. In addition to the Ardeatine Massacre, Priebke is thought to have participated in the deportation of six thousand to seven thousand Jews from Italy to the concentration camp at Auschwitz and to have tortured political prisoners. After his escape in 1945, he was not seen again until 1994. A woman doing research on Nazi war criminals in South America discovered a book, *El Pintor de la Suiza, Argentina* (*The Painter from Suiza, Argentina*), by Esteban Buch. Clues in the book led her to believe that Priebke was living in the alpine village of San Carlos de Bariloche, Argentina. He was. She dug into the matter and passed along her research to ABC TV, telling them that Priebke had been living openly in San Carlos de Bariloche and that he owned a small hotel and a delicatessen. He also was a teacher at a school there. An ABC producer convinced her to go undercover and meet with Priebke, ostensibly to discuss how she could purchase a hotel as he had done. Priebke agreed to a meeting and, during the conversation with the researcher, there was no doubt he was Erich Priebke. Days later, an ABC TV crew descended on San Carlos de Bariloche; they needed to interview Priebke on the street. Days later, ABC News reporter Sam Donaldson flew to San Carlos de Bariloche, met with the film crew, and made arrangements to film Priebke. They would wait in their cars at the school where Priebke taught. Every day at the same time, noon, he would leave the school, walk to his car, drive home for lunch, then drive back to the school.

In 1994 Priebke had no idea how much his life was about to change from obscurity to prominence throughout the world. When Priebke stepped out of the school, Donaldson and the crew swept in. We see Priebke leaving the school and walking down a sidewalk toward his Volkswagen. At any moment, we feel that Priebke is going to see the film crew approaching and bolt. (We've seen this before in TV documentaries.) Donaldson and the crew are just feet from Priebke, practically surrounding him. But then the scenario changes from pursuit to acceptance: Priebke does not run; he does not hide his face behind a newspaper or a briefcase. He simply stops on the sidewalk and, with a slight smile, stops at his car and faces Donaldson as if to say, "How can I help you?" He does not appear threatened; he is just an eighty-year-old man who seems to want to be cooperative.

Donaldson introduces himself as a correspondent for ABC News. Then he asks a direct question: "You were with the Gestapo in 1944, were you not?"

Priebke thinks for a second.

Donaldson says, "In Rome?"

Priebke calmly answers, "Yes. In Rome." He is wearing a jacket and a Tyrolean hat and could be anyone's old uncle or grandfather. There is nothing sinister about him, although he reaches for the car's door handle and obviously wants to leave. He has baleful, translucent blue eyes. It is a face that could turn sinister at any moment, like a viper. For a man his age he seems supple, slim; he walks as he would on a parade ground wearing a black uniform, straight and determined, scanning his surroundings. He does not look like a man who might suspect imminent arrest.

Donaldson asks a question about the Ardeatine Massacre that is mostly unintelligible.

Priebke doesn't even think about the answer.

He says, "Yes. I was there. You know, the Communists blew up a group of our German soldiers. They killed thirty-three. For every German soldier killed, ten civilians had to die. They had been mostly terrorists."

"But why did you shoot them?"

"No," Priebke says calmly. "We were just following orders."

"You were there in the caves?"

"Yes, of course."

"But orders are just an excuse."

"I had to obey. An order is an order. Many civilians had to die. Civilians die all over the world every day. You are living in this time, today, but that was 1944. That was different. You were not there then. We did not commit a crime. We took orders and did what we were told."

"Did you send Jews to the concentration camps?"

"Oh, no. No," says Priebke, shaking his head a bit for emphasis. "No. Not me."

Priebke manages to slide past Donaldson and his microphone and into the VW.

Just before he closes the door, we hear him say to Donaldson, "You are not a gentleman."

"I am not a gentleman?"

Priebke drives away.

When the ABC video appeared on Italian television, there was outrage. Priebke, the Gestapo man who killed two people in the Ardeatine Caves, the scorekeeper, the monster who allegedly sent thousands of Jews to the extermination camps, had been living as a free man for fifty years. He had publicly admitted his role in the murders but claimed the defense of "superior orders." Italy wanted to extradite him, but it was denied by Argentina because of a fifteen-year statute of limitations. On November 2, 1995, this ruling was reversed and Priebke was flown to Italy. He appealed and, after several years going in and out of court, was given life imprisonment. He died on October 13, 1995, in Rome—at the age of one hundred.

In Priebke's eyes the Ardeatine Massacre was not illegal; according to him and many others, it was a legal reprisal, orders that were legitimately handed down to them, orders they had to obey. Also, the Germans had been innocent victims. The partisans who killed the police had been the criminals—"terrorists," according to the Germans. Priebke claimed that they had to be punished for the deaths of thirty-three policemen. This a theme that had run throughout the war and would continue through the Nuremberg trials.

In 1967, *Death in Rome*, an Italian war drama written by Robert Katz about the Ardeatine Massacre, was made into the film *Massacre in Rome*. Directed by George Pan Cosmatos, produced by Carlo Ponti, and scripted by Cosmatos and Katz, it was a major production with well-known actors: Richard Burton played *SS-Oberturmbannführer* Herbert Kappler; Erich Priebke was portrayed by Brook Williams; Leo McKern played Luftwaffe General Kurt Mälzer, military commander of Rome; and Marcello Mastroianni played Father Pietro Antonelli. Almost as soon as the film hit theaters, Cosmatos, Ponti, and Katz were hit with a libel suit by Countess Elisabetta Pacelli Rossignani, sister of Pope Pius XII, for "defaming the memory of the Pope." The script suggested that Pope Pius XII allegedly had knowledge of the Ardeatine Massacre but did nothing about it. Katz, the author and screenwriter, was found guilty and sentenced to fourteen months in prison. Ponti and Cosmatos received sentences of six months. Soon after, the sentences were vacated.

During his trial in Venice, Field Marshal Kesselring was asked about the Ardeatine Massacre. Why did he believe that the ten-for-one reprisal ordered by Hitler's *Führerbefehl* following Via Rasella had been just?

Kesselring replied, "I thought this was a clear-cut reprisal measure. I thought that the ratio was just and fair because the outrage in Rome was extraordinary in size. There had been previous attacks [by partisans on Germans and German installations in Rome,] and the military situation demanded it."

Further questioning by Dr. Hans Laternser, a German attorney working for Kesselring, on the matter of reprisals opened a can of worms; obviously, there were several views on what constituted legal versus illegal reprisals. The result could not have pleased the prosecution:

Dr. Laternser:	Before I continue with the evidence of the witness[,] I would like to put in a document to the Court. The Court might remember that, arising out of a question of the Court, the theme was touched when it was allowed that the life of a person can be taken as a reprisal measure and the Field Marshal gave his opinion about it. Through the kindness of the American Observer[,] I got a booklet of "Rules of Warfare in the American Army," and in these rules, almost the same case is being dealt with[,] and I would like to put [into evidence its paragraph] 358, as an exhibit to the Court.
Judge Advocate:	[Interrupting] Is there any dispute between the prosecution and the defence as to what the law is?
Col. Halse:	[R. C. Halse, the prosecutor] Quite frankly as I understand it—my point is quite clear—you are entitled to take reprisals[,] but you are not entitled to take the lives of innocent people. That is my very short answer.

Judge Advocate:	But, surely, Mr. Prosecutor, you are not arguing, are you, that in the case of a reprisal it is not permissible to take the lives of perfectly innocent people?
Col. Halse:	I do not quite follow that; I am sorry.
Judge Advocate:	I want you to consider only reprisals. Is it not permissible in international law, as reprisals, to take the lives of perfectly innocent people who have had nothing to do with any particular crime at all?
Col. Halse:	I say not, it is not legal; quite definitely it is not legal to take the lives of any innocent people.
Dr. Laternser:	[Interjecting] And I say it is legal.
Judge Advocate:	Then I am quite wrong. There is a fundamental difference between the prosecution and the defense.
Dr. Laternser	Well, to help my own case in this question of fundamental disagreement between the defense and the prosecution[,] I must apply again to be allowed to put in this paragraph of American law with regard to land warfare[,] which says quite clearly that, in a reprisal, you are entitled to take the lives even of innocent people[,] and I would like to emphasize that the conditions under which you are entitled to take the lives of innocent people are exactly the same which the Field Marshal laid down in his order [relating to Charge II;] they are the same here in this booklet concerning American laws of land warfare.
Judge Advocate:	Mr. Prosecutor, where do you get your authority for the statement that, supposing you cannot find the actual perpetrator of the offence, you cannot take a reprisal against innocent people? It is quite clear you can take a reprisal against innocent people in some way, is it not? Surely you agree that a reprisal can be taken against a perfectly innocent person.
Col. Halse:	I entirely agree.
Judge Advocate:	Are you drawing a distinction that that reprisal cannot take the form of an execution?

Col. Halse:	Yes; there are certain circumstances, I agree, when possibly—I say "possibly"—an innocent life might be taken as a reprisal.
Judge Advocate:	But you have just said the very contrary.
Col. Halse:	But I say as a rule an innocent life cannot be taken as a reprisal.
Judge Advocate:	I put to you quite clearly that there was a fundamental difference between you and the defence and you agree, and that the defense's contention was that[,] in a proper case[,] a reprisal could extend to the killing of an innocent person. I thought you said your view was quite the contrary[,] and that you could not kill innocent people by way of a reprisal.
Col. Halse:	That is what I said.
Judge Advocate:	I thought you were weakening from that and saying in some cases you agree.
Col. Halse:	I am sorry if you misunderstood me. My case is that you cannot take the lives of innocent people by way of a reprisal.
Judge Advocate:	Are you prepared later on to give the court some legal authority on that?
Col. Halse:	I am prepared to argue that case, yes.
Judge Advocate:	But you will agree that there can be no question at all that you can have a reprisal, a sort of execution, against innocent persons?
Col. Halse:	It is quite clear that there can be reprisal taken which would affect innocent people, burning of houses and so on and so forth, and during such reprisal an innocent person might lose his life[,] but I say it is quite illegal[,] during a reprisal[,] by execution to kill an innocent person. I make the distinction between a reprisal being taken against an area[,] such as a bombing from the air where undoubtedly innocent people—it must be after a warning—where undoubtedly innocent people might lose their lives, and the

deliberate execution of innocent people. I say the former might be legal, the latter certainly not.

Judge Advocate: I thought, Mr. Prosecutor, the point you were directing us to was whether[,] when a reprisal was taken by way of execution[,] the number of people killed[,] for instance[,] was appropriate and not excessive in the sense of being an abuse of international law; I thought this was [going to be your] point.

Col. Halse: Well, that is another point. That is another part of my argument, that the reprisals[,] if taken[,] must be [proportionate to what the enemy suffered, and I still say, and my argument is going to be, that you cannot take the lives of innocent people deliberately.

The following is an excerpt from the American Observer booklet entitled *The Rules of Land Warfare*, which deals with reprisals:

[Par] 358: Reprisals: (a): Definition: Reprisals are acts of retaliation resorted to by one belligerent against the enemy individual or property for illegal acts of warfare committed by the other belligerent, for the purpose of enforcing future compliance with the recognized rules of civilized warfare. 9b). When and how employed Reprisals are never adopted merely for revenge, but only as unavoidable last resort to induce the enemy to desist from illegitimate practices. They should never be employed by individual soldiers except by direct orders of a commander, and the latter should give such orders only after careful enquiry into the alleged offense.

On February 7, 1947, Lt. General John Harding, Comm, Central Mediterranean Force, ordered the convention of a British Military Court to try German Prisoner of War *Generalfeldmarschall* (Field Marshal) Albert Konrad Kesselring for war crimes committed under his command in Italy in the summer of 1944. Two charges were specified:

CHARGE 1: [that he] AT ROME, ITALY on or about 23 March 1944, in violation of the laws and usages of war, was concerned in the killing as a reprisal some 335 Italian Nationals in the Ardeatine Caves; and CHARGE II: [that he, between JUNE and August 1944, in violation of the laws and usages of war, when OBERBEFEHLSLABER [*sic*] der HEEREGRUPPE [*sic*] SOUTHWEST COMMANDER-IN-CHIEF ARMY GROUP SOUTH WEST) [*sic*] incited and commanded the German Army Force and German Police Forces in ITALY under his command to kill Italian Civilians as reprisal in consequence of which a number of Italian Civilians were killed.

There was also a Charge III, which has little to do with this narrative.

At 1000 hours on February 10, Kesselring was taken to the *Tribunale di Giustizia* (Court of Justice) in Venice, Italy, where he was arraigned and pleaded not guilty; he was granted a stay of seven days.

Between March 3 and March 11, he was examined and cross-examined. As has been stated before, he repeatedly testified—as did his staff—that he had visited the Cassino front from sunrise to sunset on March 23, 1944, and then flown back to his headquarters at Monte Soratte, north of Rome, that same day. When he arrived at dusk, his adjutant told him about the Via Rasella attack, that no assassins had been apprehended, and that Hitler had been notified and was in a rage. Hitler, in his order, had proposed a reprisal of ten Italian citizens for one German policeman killed. Coincidentally, minutes later, *SS-Obersturmbannführer* Herbert Kappler, Gestapo chief in Rome, spoke on the phone with the field marshal and advised him that a sufficient number of Italians who had earlier been sentenced to death were available for the reprisal executions; therefore, no innocents needed to be executed. Almost simultaneously, Hitler's *Führerbefehl* arrived at Kesselring's headquarters at Monte Soratte from Supreme Armed Forces Headquarters (*Oberkommando der Wehrmacht,* or OKW)—this was an order from Hitler that had to be obeyed immediately. Kesselring admitted that he had instructed Westphal to pass the order along to AOK, the German Fourteenth Army (*Armeeoberkommando 14,* or AOK 14), which had to carry out the executions.

Around midnight, Kesselring had gone to bed. Immediately follow-ing this, Westphal had received a second *Führerbefehl*. Again, Westphal went to Kesselring, who instructed him to pass it along to AOK 14, which he did.

At dawn on March 24, Kesselring said, he flew again to Cassino. He denied that he had been informed of the second *Führerbefehl* until he returned to Monte Soratte, late on March 24 or possibly the evening of March 25.

Over and over, Kesselring repeated his testimony regarding the all-important dates of March 23 and 24, 1944. This can be seen in a direct examination by Dr. Laternser, Kesselring's attorney:

Dr. Laternser: When you returned from a front line visit and you re-turned to your general headquarters [on Monte Sorat-te] how was that reported to the various offices?

Kesselring: The whole staff was nearly always in a state of emer-gency because it was generally very late when I returned to my headquarters[,] and the latest would be that the guard would report by phone that I am coming.

The President: [Interrupting] As far as you remember could you say at what time you returned on the night of 23rd March 1944 from this front line visit to your general headquar-ters?

Kesselring: As far as I remember between 1900 and 2000 hours.

When cross-examined by the prosecutor, Colonel Halse, Kesselring swore he had visited the southern front on March 23. In response, Halse asked: "When did you first learn that some policemen had been killed in the Via Rasella?" Kesselring responded, "When I returned on the evening of 23rd March from the front line; that was between 1900 hours and 2000 hours."

The President of the Court then questioned Kesselring regarding his location on 23 and 24 March, and it engendered this testimony:

The President: I am sorry to go back to [23 and 24 March] again[,] but the court wants to clear up the sequence of events if

	possible. What was your usual custom when you visited the front; how did you get the last situation before you left your headquarters? Would an officer report to you or did you visit the map room, the maps in the office? How did you get a final picture of the situation before you left your headquarters to visit the front normally?
Kesselring:	In normal times every morning whilst I had my breakfast[,] all the news reports which had come in during the night were brought to me[,] and sometimes my chief of staff again in the morning was present and told me quite shortly what had happened.
The President:	Did that happen whenever you left for the front?
Kesselring:	Yes, and I never left without having a conversation with a responsible officer about the situation.
The President:	Can we assume that that happened on the morning of the 24th March?
Kesselring:	Yes, I think I should like to assume it.
The President:	Then before you left on the morning of the 24th March[,] a responsible officer came in and gave you a picture of the front?
Kesselring:	I should think that did happen.
The President:	But presumably on that day[,] neither Beelitz nor Westphal?
Kesselring:	I cannot say.
The President:	When you came back on the night of the 23rd—you told us you came back on the night of the 23rd about 2000 hours—and you then went to bed about 2200 hours/2300 hours, and you got up at four or five o'clock on the morning of the 24th. When did you give the orders to have the cars and vehicle ready to take you away on the 24th?
Kesselring:	Certainly before I went to bed.
The President:	So you had made up your mind before you went to bed that[,] provided something unforeseen did not occur

during the morning[,] that we were going to leave the morning very early for the [Cassino] front?

Westphal also testified that Kesselring had been at Cassino on March 23 and had returned to Monte Soratte that evening.

Col. Halse:	[To Westphal] Where was the Field Marshal on 23 March 1944?
Westphal:	On 10 Army (Cassino) front.
Col. Halse:	Where did he go during the day?
Westphal:	I do not know where he was in detail; I rather imagine he was with Fourteen Panzer Corps on the Cassino front.
Col. Halse:	Why do you think he was with Fourteen Panzer Corps?
Westphal:	Because Fourteen Panzer Corps always led where the main effort was [on that front.]
Col. Halse:	When did you expect the Field Marshal to return on 23rd March?
Westphal:	In the evening when twilight had started.
....	
Col. Halse:	Did you know he was coming back that night [23 March]?
Westphal:	Yes, as far as one could suppose by normal human methods[,] he would be back.
Col. Halse:	How did you know he was coming back that night?
Westphal:	Probably he had said so in the morning?
....	
Col. Halse:	Did you know the Field Marshal was coming back on 23rd March?
Westphal:	No, when I came back from [Civita Castellan] I asked *Oberst* Beelitz whether we could get into touch with the Field Marshal[,] and[,] as they told me they could not

get in touch with him[,] had to assume he was on his way back.

. . . .

Col. Halse: How long would it have taken the Field Marshal to get back to your headquarters from the front?

Westphal: Two hours if he had used the Stork; if he did not use the Stork[,] three or four hours.

Col. Halse: Did he use the Stork [on 23 March]?

Westphal: As far as I remember, yes.

Col. Halse: What is the last possible time he could have left the [landing field at Frosinone, fifty kilometers north of Cassino] in order to get back to your headquarters for landing?

Westphal: 1700 hours, roughly that is.

Col. Halse: That is the last possible time?

Westphal: Yes, assuming of course all the time that it was not summertime then.

Col. Halse: We add another hour if it was summertime? [In 1944, German summertime did not come into effect until April.]

Westphal: Yes.

Kesselring, as he had done numerous times in the past, claimed that his only role in the Ardeatine Massacre had been to *pass along* to AOK 14 the reprisal order demanded by Hitler that had resulted in the execution of criminals already sentenced to death.

This is an important aspect of this narrative, because it was pivotal to Kesselring's defense and because it relates to the Ginny OGs' execution as well.

Here is unequivocal proof that among Kesselring's staff, there was a "conspiracy to shoot" and to shield their field marshal—and essentially lie to the courts about their whereabouts. A cover-up was afoot, and Kesselring got away with his life because of it.

Oberst (Colonel) Dietrich Beelitz, Kesselring's chief of staff, supported Kesselring's claim that he and Westphal had been at Cassino on March 23. When Kesselring and Westphal were away, Beelitz was in complete control of Kesselring's headquarters at Monte Soratte. Westphal likewise stated that Kesselring had been at Cassino on March 23, returning on March 24.

Dr. Laternser, Kesselring's defense lawyer, and prosecutor Colonel Halse delivered their closings on April 10, 1947. The trial ended after its fifty-ninth day.

Kesselring's testimony ended on Saturday, April 26, 1947, at 1230 hours.

The court spent little time deliberating. When it reconvened at 0945 hours, it announced to Kesselring that it had found him guilty on both charges. The court adjourned briefly to deliberate the sentence. The court then announced its sentence to the defendant: "The sentence which the court has passed upon you is that you suffer death by being shot."

AFTERWORD

In this book we have concentrated on Operation Ginny and two seemingly unrelated events: the Via Rasella attack in Rome, and the Ardeatine Massacre the following day, in which more than three hundred civilians were killed with shots to the back of the head at the Ardeatine Caves. All three events took place over the same span of days: Operation Ginny between March 22 and 27, 1944; the Via Rasella bombing attack on 142 German policemen on March 23; and the Ardeatine Massacre, the Germans' reprisal for the Via Rasella bombing occurring on the afternoon and evening of March 24.

The link, the one constant among these events, is *Generalfeldmarschall* (General Field Marshal) Albert Kesselring, who lied about his involvement in the three events. In the end, his lies worked. Kesselring was found guilty in the Ardeatine Massacre case (although the proof was tenuous) and sentenced to death, a sentence that was later commuted. For this, he felt lucky. He knew that if he had been charged and found guilty of the execution of the Ginny OGs, he would have been executed. He correctly concluded that since the Americans would be trying him for the Ginny deaths, the prosecutor would be out for revenge. An American trial would be seeking punishment, not necessarily justice. The coincidence of the dates could not have been better for Kesselring: He needed only one excuse to cover all three incidents in order to escape the gallows. "Smilin' Al" had served himself well.

In the Ardeatine Massacre trial, Kesselring was accused of murdering more than three hundred Italians. His defense was, like Dostler's, that he had merely obeyed Hitler's *Führerbefehl*—essentially obeying Hitler and, therefore, the civil laws of Nazi Germany.

On January 30, 1933, President Paul von Hindenburg had appointed Hitler chancellor of Germany and Führer, making him the legal head of state accountable to the laws of Germany and its constitution. Kesselring was saying that the reprisal at Ardeatine had resulted from Hitler's legal order as head of state per international law, German civil law, and an urgent military decision that had been passed down to Kesselring.

Kesselring stated, "I never issued orders which were contrary either to the laws or usage of war, and those alleged happenings cannot be represented as originating because of my order."

He went on to quote *The Rules of Land Warfare*, which we mentioned earlier regarding reprisals, legal or otherwise, which states: "Hostages . . . may be punished or put to death if illegal actions are nevertheless committed and allowed summary execution of guerrillas or partisans." He also said that every German soldier's pay book stated that "spies and partisans should not be executed but brought before a court-martial."

At his trial, Kesselring proffered that in the case of the Ardeatine Massacre, the responsibility ultimately lay with Hitler, who, as Supreme Commander, had issued a legal order through his *Führerbefehl*. Thus, the *Führerbefehl* was a lawful order, a binding order, and, like all orders, it had to be obeyed, no questions asked. In any event, it was not the soldier's duty to question an order—*"Befehl ist Befehl"* ("an order is an order"). Kesselring said the Germans felt that any legal order issued had to be obeyed without question. In fact, in SS-Gestapo Chief Herbert Kappler's Italian trial, the Italians accepted the legality of that order. Kesselring asserted that at the time of the Ardeatine Massacre, he was a German, subject to German law—and not obliged to follow a newly imposed "Anglo-Saxon version" of statutes for the German Army. We believe he was correct. Anything Kesselring did was done within the boundaries of German civil law, German military law, and military regulations. We believe that no other countries could or should have been allowed to impose their laws on Germany and its soldiers. But the Americans and British were saying, "You lost the war, we won the war, and now we do what we want." This thinking was taken into the Nuremberg trials. The bottom line was:

"Don't lose a war. If you do, you are subject to the victor's rules, their regulations, and their viewpoints." Victory, it seems, gives license to the victor to do what they want—even if it includes the imposition of their laws and a thirst for vengeance.

The field marshal added: "In extraordinary emergency cases, I, as supreme commander, had the right to order those reprisals should be taken and could disregard the whole legal machinery." To an extent, Kesselring was right. He and every German soldier in service had taken the *Führereid* (Führer Oath) on August 2, 1934:

> I swear to God this holy oath
> that I shall render unconditional obedience
> to the Leader of the German Reich and people,
> Adolf Hitler, supreme commander of the armed forces,
> and that as a brave soldier, I shall at all times be prepared
> to give my life for this oath.

What is the sense of taking an oath if it is okay to disobey that oath? The answer can only be: None.

When Hitler issued the *Führerbefehl* on October 18, 1942, Kesselring and every soldier that day had taken the *Führereid*, which obliged them to obey the *Führerbefehl*. Anton Dostler, when asked about disobeying the *Führerbefehl*, told the court that he knew of only three general officers who had defied the order and that they had been severely punished (he did not specify the punishment). Their understanding of the Führer Order, their loyalty to the Führer, and their oath of allegiance led them to believe that the reprisal deaths at the Ardeatine Caves and the executions of the Ginny OGs at Punta Bianca were perfectly legal. For both, there was no ambiguity—except for Dostler, who had hesitated and rescinded his order to execute in order to "cover his ass." He was waiting to hear from Colonel Kraehe, von Zangen's chief of staff.

The Italians believed that the Germans were in Italy illegally and, as such, were the enemy. In the minds of the Italians, this allowed them to act against the Germans on Via Rasella and kill as many policemen as possible.

◦—◦

"War," Sir Winston Churchill said, "is mainly a catalog of blunders."

So it was with both Ginnys. Blunders and miscalculations—some bigger than others—caused the failure of both operations.

On February 27, 1944, Ginny I stuttered to a start and never recovered, provoking an aborted mission and ultimate failure. Ginny II, the follow-up operation known simply as Ginny, was an even greater failure because it resulted in the deaths of the fifteen OSS men who undertook the mission believing they stood a chance of succeeding. However, even the planners had thought the mission would be "risky."

In each operation, the failures were the operators' own doing. A fisherman in his boat quickly spotted the ineffectually camouflaged rubber boats, and the boats' bright orange color was an inexcusable choice for "blending in."

After landing, Lt. Vincent Russo, commander of the OGs, approached a young boy and asked for food and directions—an inexcusable error, because Russo had no idea where the boy's allegiance lay or if he would report the OGs to the Germans or Fascists. It is safe to assume that Russo had no notion of what the *Kommandobefehl von 18 Oktober 1942* had prescribed for him and his men should they be captured—that it contained an order for execution. Perhaps if he did, he and his men might have tried to shoot their way out instead of allowing themselves to be captured.

Dostler knew, because he was familiar with the *Führerbefehl*, what the sole criterion for execution was: The Ginny OGs had been captured behind the lines; they were on a mission, and it made no difference that they were in the uniforms of the US Army and hadn't resisted capture. Further, the Supplement to the *Führerbefehl* clearly stated that commandos would be turned over to the SD for what we know was a death sentence.

Before the *Führerbefehl*, the Germans knew that if commandos surrendered, they would be treated as POWs and taken to a POW camp. After the Supplement, commandos would not be allowed to surrender as POWs; instead they would be executed.

A short time after the OGs vainly attempted to conceal them, their orange rubber boats were discovered. A group of Fascists and Germans later engaged the OGs in a brief firefight. Russo surrendered the group, and that afternoon, March 24, they were taken to *Oberst* (Colonel) Almers's headquarters, where intense interrogations began. It was Almers's understanding of a published Führer Order that the captured OGs, "members of the 'so-called Commandos,' either in uniform or in civilian clothes were to be eliminated." This of course is a reference to the *Führer befehl*. One of the interrogators voiced the opposite view: "The so-called Commandos were to be treated as POWs." That night, March 24, the interrogators were told that the Commando Order applied to the OGs and that they were to be shot at 0500 hours the following day. General Dostler's order was finalized by late afternoon—the OGs were to be executed the next day. On March 27 the OGs were lined up at Punta Bianca, executed, and buried in a common grave.

According to von Zangen, Dostler was unwilling to order the execution until *Oberst* (Colonel) Horst Kraehe, von Zangen's chief of staff at Headquarters LXXV Army Corps, obtained confirmation from the next higher echelon, *Armee-Gruppe von Zangen*. However, von Zangen claimed he was not at his headquarters. Instead, Colonel Walter Nagel, von Zangen's chief of staff, relayed Dostler's request upward to *Heeresgruppe*.

In Dostler's sworn statement after the war, he seems certain that Kesselring was the higher authority who authorized the Ginny executions (something Kesselring would deny). However, this was difficult to prove conclusively.

It seems implausible, too, that the OSS's Research and Analysis branch in 1944, many years into the war, had no knowledge, even superficially, of the *Führerbefehl*. One German general stated after the war that he believed the *Führerbefehl* had been sent to the Allies, warning them what was in store if their commandos were caught—in essence, giving them a "heads up." It seems implausible, even unacceptable, that OSS was not aware of Hitler's penchant for executing saboteurs. A US Armed Forces communiqué of March 7, 1942, broadcast throughout Europe via Radio Berlin, stated, "In [the] future, all terror and sabotage troops of the British and their accomplices, who do not behave as soldiers but rather as bandits, will be treated in the same way by German troops and, where they behave that way, will be ruthlessly slain in combat." On March 8, 1942, the notice was published in the *New York Times*.

And there is the difference between Dostler, Kesselring, and Mỹ Lai: Dostler and Kesselring took their actions under the full sanction of their government. The Mỹ Lai massacre was wholesale criminality.

But Dostler did finally issue the order, and the court found him guilty and sentenced him to death. However, many American officers, generals in particular, did not want to find themselves in Dostler's shoes had they lost the war.

Unquestionably, every nation has the right to raise an army for the protection of its borders and its people. Within that army are rules and laws applicable to their conduct. Kesselring said that at the time of the Ardeatine Massacre, he was a German, subject to German law—not obliged to a newly imposed "Anglo-Saxon version" of statutes for the German Army. Dostler knew that when he finally issued the OGs' execution order, he had the full endorsement of his army, his government, and its laws. He did so with a clear conscience, believing he was acting legally according to the rules he had sworn numerous times to obey.

Kesselring's guilt in the Ardeatine Massacre was tenuous. There was no hard-core evidence to prove unquestionably that he had ordered the killings at Ardeatine, but the thirst for punishment and revenge leading up to his trial—and the trial itself—was enough to find him guilty. He was sentenced to death, but that sentence was later commuted. As a field marshal, Kesselring had the authority to approve or disapprove endorsement of the *Kommandobefehl*—but he too was bound by the laws of his nation.

Imagine if the tables had been turned and the Americans had lost the war. The Americans would surely have objected to the German government imposing German military law on their troops.

The climate after the war's end in 1945 was, unquestionably, one of retribution. Justice was veiled and took a back seat, and this was quite apparent at the time. Punishment was pursued more vigorously than justice. This thinking and attitude would extend to Nuremberg, where the results of Operation Ginny would have a significant impact on the proceedings. There, many aspects of Operation Ginny were precedent-setting and de rigueur from the beginning of the trials to the closing gavel.

The refrain of "superior orders," "just following orders," and the more rigid German "*Befehl ist Befehl*" was part of every day's testimony. It was the standard defense.

We do not believe Anton Dostler should have been executed. He wasn't being judged, he was being punished. His trial had been less than perfect. If you recall, he had been denied two witnesses.

"In war," Winston Churchill said, "the laws are silent."

General Telford Taylor stated: "War consists largely of acts that would be criminal if performed in time of peace—killing, wounding, destroying, or carrying off other people's property. Such conduct is not regarded as criminal if it takes place in the course of war because the state of war lays a blanket of immunity over warriors."

Today, the necessity to clearly define "superior orders" has still not been adequately defined. If taken at face value that Dostler was guilty of obeying an illegal order, then why weren't the truck drivers who drove the OGs to Punta Bianca also guilty of their deaths? The riflemen who shot them not charged with their deaths? All of them were obeying orders.

The question becomes: "Are the subordinate commanders and soldiers of the firing squad guilty of war crimes when they are carrying out orders of colonels and generals? The latter, if apprehended, will probably say they got orders from the higher-ups."

This is not a forum to alter the definition of "superior orders" or an "order is an order" and who might, in the chain of events, be guilty of issuing and obeying an order. The question now might be: "Where does the illegality begin and where does it end?" Because now, the question lacks clarity.

BIBLIOGRAPHY

Adams, Henry Hitch. *Italy at War.* Chicago: Time-Life Books, Inc., 1982.

Angolia, John R. Ltc. (Ret.). *For Fuehrer and Fatherland: Military Awards of the Third Reich.* San Jose, CA: R. James Bender Publishing, 1985.

———. *Insignia of the Third Reich: Cloth Badges and Emblems.* San Jose, CA: R. James Bender Publishing, 1974.

———. *The Luftwaffe: Air Organizations of the Third Reich.* San Jose, CA: R. James Bender Publishing, 1972.

———, assisted by Stan Cook. *Cloth Insignia of the SS.* San Jose, CA: R. James Bender Publishing, 1983.

Bailey, Ronald H. *Partisans and Guerrillas.* Alexandria, VA: Time-Life Books Inc, 1978.

Brown, Anthony Cave. *Wild Bill Donovan: The Last Hero.* New York: New York Times Books, 1982.

Browning, Christopher R. *Ordinary Men: Reserve Police Battalion 101 and the Final Solution in Poland.* Eastbourne, UK: Gardners Books, 2001.

Bureau of Ships. *Know Your PT Boat.* Washington, DC: Navy Department, 1945.

Code Name, Operations of WWII. *Operation Ginny.*

Dostler Case. Case No. 2. *Trial of General Anton Dostler, Commander of the 75th German Army Corps.* United States Military Commission, Rome, 8th–12th October, 1945.

Fisher, Ernest F., Jr. *Cassino to the Alps: United States Army in World War II. Mediterranean Theater of Operations.* Washington, DC: USGPRO, 1977.

Führer Directives and Other Top-Level Directives of the German Armed Force, 1939–1941, Vol. 1. Berlin: Bernard & Graefe, 1959.

Hayes, A. *SS Uniforms, Insignia & Accoutrements: A Study in Photographs.* Atglen, PA: Schiffer Military History, 2004.

Katz, Robert. *Death in Rome.* New York: Macmillan, 1967.

Macksey, Kenneth. *Kesselring: German Master of the Second World War.* London: Greenhill Books, 1996.

Margry, Karel. "The Dostler Case." *After the Battle* 96 (1996).

Miller, Russell. *The Commandos.* Chicago: Time-Life Books, Inc., 1981.

Moran, Pat, and Jon McGuire. *German Headgear in World War II; SS, MSDP, Police, Civilian, & Misc: A Photographic Study of German Hats and Helmets.* Atglen, PA: Schiffer Military History, 1997.

O'Donnell, Patrick. *Operatives, Spies, and Saboteurs: The Unknown Story of the Men and Women of WWII's OSS.* Free Press reprint edition, 2014.

OSS Weapons. *Special Weapons and Devices, Research and Development Branch, Office of Strategic Services,* Washington, DC, June 1944.

"The Peers Inquiry of the Massacre at My Lai." https://www.loc.gov/collections/military-legal-resources/?q=pdf/Law-Reports_Vol-1.pdf.

Raiber, Richard. *Anatomy of Perjury: Field Marshal Albert Kesselring, Via Rasella, and the Ginny Mission.* University of Delaware Press, 2008.

Report of the Department of the Army Review of the Preliminary Investigations into the Mỹ Lai Incident. Volume 1: The Report of the Investigation. December 10, 1974. https://www.loc.gov/collections/military-legal-resources/?q=pdf/Law-Reports_Vol-1.pdf.

Report of the Ginny II Operation. https://docs.google.com/viewer?a=v&pid=sites&srcid=ZGVmYXVsdGRvbWFpbnxvc3NvcGVyYXRpb25hbGdyb3Vwc3xneDozNzJhZGU2NGUzYjU1MGZk.

Roosevelt, Kermit. *War Report of the OSS.* New York: Walker and Company, 1976.

Smart, Don. *Top Secret: OSS Operation Ginny Met with a Tragic End during the Italian Campaign.* https://warfarehistorynetwork.com/2019/01/04/top-secret-oss-operation-ginny.

Stone, David. *Hitler's Army: The Men, Machines, and Organization, 1939–1945*. Minneapolis: Zenith Press, 2009.

Taylor, Telford. *The Anatomy of the Nuremberg Trials: A Personal Memoir*. New York: Knopf, 1992.

Thomas, Nigel. Illustrated by Stephen Andrew. *The German Army 1939–45 (5)*. Osprey Publishing.

Trials of the German War Criminals Before the International Military Tribunal, Nuremberg, 14 November 1945–1 October 1946. Vol. 9, 21–22. Nuremberg, 1948.

US Department of the Army. *Explosives and Demolitions. Field Manual, FM 5-25*. Washington, DC: Headquarters, Department of the Army, February 1971.

United Nations War Crimes Commission. *Law Reports of Trials of War Criminals. Volume 8, Case No. 44*. Washington, DC: Central Intelligence Agency, Center for the Study of Intelligence, 1981.

Wikipedia. "Anton Dostler." https://en.wikipedia.org/wiki/Anton_Dostler.

———. "Anton Dostler." https://military-history.fandom.com/wiki/Anton_Dostler.

———. "Ardeatine Massacre." https://en.wikipedia.org/wiki/Ardeatine_massacre.

———. "Herbert Kappler." https://en.wikipedia.org/wiki/Herbert_Kappler.

———. "Kurt Mälzer." https://en.wikipedia.org/wiki/Kurt_M%C3%A4lzer.

———. "Mỹ Lai Massacre." https://en.wikipedia.org/wiki/M%E1%BB%B9_Lai_massacre.

———. "Via Rasella Attack." https://en.wikipedia.org/wiki/Ardeatine_massacre tps://en.wikipedia.org/wiki/Via_Rasella_attack.

Williamson, Gordon. Illustrated by Malcolm McGregor. *German Commanders of World War II (2); Waffen-SS, Luftwaffe & Navy*. Oxford: Osprey Publishing, 2006.

———. Illustrated by Ramiro Bujeiro. *Knight's Cross with Diamonds Recipients: 1941–45*. Oxford: Osprey Publishing, 2006.

INDEX

Note: Page numbers P-1 to P-8 indicate pages of the photo insert.